WARREN, MARY,

I hope you
enjoy my book.

THE END
of LAWYERS:

Thank Goodness!

Estate Planning &
The End of Inefficient Lawyers

by

Jamie Hargrove
Attorney, CPA
NetLaw Co-Founder

Contributing Author:
Roger Madden
Attorney, LL.M in Taxation
NetLaw Co-Founder

Jamie Hargrove
12910 Shelbyville Road, Suite 124
Louisville, KY 40243

www.EndofLawyers.com

This book is not intended to offer any tax, legal, financial or investment advice and is further not
intended as a substitute for the legal advice that may be given by an attorney. The reader should
consult with an attorney relative to legal matters.

Ordering Information:

Quantity sales. Special discounts are available on quantity purchases by corporations,
associations, and others. For details, contact the publisher at the address above.

Orders by U.S. trade bookstores and wholesalers. Please contact
Case Russell Publishing, LLC:
www.CaseRussell.com or www.EndofLawyers.com.

ISBN: 978-1-889937-20-5

Cover Design by Andy Horner, Atlanta, Georgia
Book Design & Production by Karen Alsup, Louisville, Kentucky
Editing provided by Amy Higgs, Louisville, Kentucky
Authors photographs by Phillips L. Mitchell, Lexington, Kentucky
Audio Book recorded by C. L. "Lee" Rutherford, Lexington, Kentucky

Printed in the United States of America
by Four Colour Print Group, Louisville, Kentucky.

Acknowledgments

Launching and raising capital for NetLaw®, keeping up with my law practice at Hargrove Madden, finding time for family and church responsibilities and writing this book have been a fairly significant undertaking. Even with the blessing of an above-average level of energy, there have been times my workload seemed a bit over the top. My only means of survival has been the key people in my life who are my life support in each of these important areas.

So first off, thanks to Renee, the love of my life. I truly appreciate Renee, my wife of almost 32 years, for all she does to support me, to love me. I was a lot to put up with before I added NetLaw and this book to our life. So, thanks Renee!

I also want to thank our wonderful kids, Alex, Seth, Tucker and Lily for their support and encouragement. And special thanks go to my son Alex. Without his brilliance and persistence during the early years of NetLaw (and continuing today) there wouldn't be a NetLaw, and without NetLaw, I probably never would've had the motivation to write this book. And while we are talking about NetLaw, thanks to the 20+ investors in NetLaw for their almost $7 million investment and for believing not just in a fantastic business plan and exciting business model but more importantly for believing in me. Of particular significance with any start-up is your first investor The $1 million initial investment by Davis Marksbury was that significance for me. For NetLaw, I will always appreciate Davis' trust and support of me by making that initial significant start-up investment and his continued involvement on our board.

Parents always play a role in our lives, and certainly mine have done that. My mom, Sue Hargrove, and my dad, Robert Hargrove (deceased) have impacted every aspect of my life. My mom's wisdom and humor and my dad's hard work and engineer mind (and humor) along with their continuous support laid a foundation that was absolutely key. And thanks to Tim and Brad for being the best brothers I could ask for. With my practice, too often I see conflict and strife among family members. I am thankful that our family has avoided any hint of family conflict or strife. Thanks to Tim and Brad for their sense of humor, support and interest in my work and their willingness to support our mom at times when I might be too busy to do my fair share.

Thanks to my law partners at Hargrove Madden (Roger Madden, Melissa Stewart and Jamie Traughber) and all the others at the firm who have so supported me and my part of the practice during these challenging but fulfilling years of the NetLaw start-up. Something had to give, and what gave was everyone at the firm picking up the slack to support these extra initiatives. And, of course, without my assistant, Stephanie Portell, I never would have been able to juggle all the balls I have thrown into the air.

I also particularly appreciate Roger and his 17-plus years of practicing with me. He is as solid as a rock: savvy businessman, talented lawyer with phenomenal judgment and common sense, and just a really great guy. Our vision for NetLaw is now taking root and his key involvement there, particularly in the early days of its development, has been critical to the success of the company. This book only made sense, resting upon the foundation of a successful law practice. Plus, Roger's help with this book was significant and has added greatly to the end product.

Of course, a word of thanks goes to the great leadership team assembled at NetLaw. NetLaw is a phenomenal company with an unbelievable opportunity in the marketplace. Without the support and encouragement of Mark Sisk, NetLaw's President and COO, this book could have never been completed. Thanks also to Charlsey Baumeier, the sole survivor (other than Roger and me) of the early start-up days when NetLaw was still part of the law firm. I also want to thank fellow NetLaw employee Beverly Rawlings. Bev was an estate planning paralegal for me during the major growth of Roger's and my practice in the 1990s. She later returned to play a significant role in NetLaw. Her extra set of eyes to polish and fine-tune this book was very beneficial. Thanks also to the rest of the current NetLaw team.

Thanks to Ted Renaker and Gary Grosenick, the partners of the international accounting firm of Alexander Grant & Co. (now Grant Thornton) for giving me my first job. They not only gave me my first job out of law school, they promoted me like crazy. I was the only CPA/attorney practicing as a CPA in Lexington at the time, and being the great marketers they were, they used that to their advantage and, of course, to mine. It was with this firm that I first learned the importance of systems and processes, and it was there that I was able to start learning about computers and programming. From Ted, in particular, I learned how to market myself and the firm, how to make clients better appreciate professional services and how to always deliver quality.

I also want to acknowledge some of my past law partners, without whom my career and practice would not have reached their current level. No doubt the success that Roger and I have had with growing our law practice and the reputation of the firm are due in part to some great partnerships over the past three decades.

First, thanks to the partners at Fowler Measle & Bell for giving me my first law job and allowing me to serve as their tax attorney for almost five years. Tommy Bell, Guy Colson, Taft McKinstry, Pat Moores, Walter Cox and John Hinkle were among the partners there to encourage a young attorney. I will always remember my first firm meeting, when it was announced by the firm's managing partner that "from this point forward, any and all estate planning will be handled by Jamie Hargrove." Those words had hardly come out of Walter Cox's mouth when Mr. Bell said under his breath (but for all to hear), "What's he know about estate planning?" That was June of 1985. I was two years out of law school and while I had practiced in public accounting for two years, I had never practiced law. So clearly, Mr. Bell was right. I didn't know enough to be designated as the firm's expert, and no doubt the other partners probably agreed. But everyone recognized I was going to be the firm's future when it came to estate planning, and they were willing to take a chance on me and put their confidence and trust in me to make sure I worked hard enough to figure it out. For over four years, I was strongly promoted by the partners and supported by the firm. For that, I am very grateful.

Thanks to Jim Newberry and Bill Rambicure and a host of other very smart and talented partners at Newberry, Hargrove & Rambicure for allowing me to be an entrepreneur and spend money on technology, systems and people to grow my practice during the 1990s. What a great experience to grow our three-person start-up to almost 30 attorneys, and a very impressive who's who list of attorneys to boot. A special thanks to Jim Newberry for his serving as the Managing Partner of Hargrove Madden in 2011-12 and helping expand the law firm into 23 states with over 30 attorneys. Also thanks to the role Kevin Ghassomian and Heather Flanagan played during those days of crazy expansion of the law firm and development of our online practice that the American Bar Association recognized in early 2012 as being the best delivery of online legal services of any law firm of any kind anywhere in the U.S.

Thanks also to my former partners at Frost Brown Todd, who were also always very supportive. There are too many to name, but Paul Sullivan's leadership in recruiting me gave me the "big-firm" experience that was another strong building block in my practice.

And finally, the most recent firm, where I was a partner for close to nine years, Stoll Keenon Ogden. They played an important role in allowing Roger's and my practice to explode. The practice almost tripled in size and profitability during those years. The support of the firm and its managing partner for several of those years, Bill Lear, was tremendous. Even when Roger and I decided to roll out our practice into what is now Hargrove Madden, so many of the partners of SKO remained supportive and encouraging. I will always remember the SKO Christmas party just before Roger and our team departed the firm. As I talked about my vision for a 50-state online estate planning practice, what seemed to be a dozen or more of the SKO partners listened with great interest and encouragement, and almost every one of them made the statement, "Well, Jamie, if anybody can do it, you can do it!"

Renee and I are both graduates of Western Kentucky University. What a great place, and what a wonderful place of challenge and encouragement to me as a student there. Former WKU presidents, Dr. Dero Downing and Dr. Donald Zacharias, both now deceased, were such great encouragers. What a great opportunity as a rural Kentuckian for me to be able to be a student representative on the WKU Board of Regents and have the opportunity to know these two great leaders. Also at WKU (and even continuing now) thanks to Dr. Randall Capps as a professor, mentor and now professional advisor and friend. Also thanks to Gary Ransdell, WKU President now for close to 20 years, for his leadership at WKU and friendship that have combined to be impactful on multiple fronts.

Law school took me to Lexington to the University of Kentucky College of Law. And once again a place of great encouragement was central to the experience. Before my wonderful secondary and post-secondary education was my high school experience at Trimble County High School. Teachers, like my math teacher for 4 years, Dean Bowling, a teacher and basketball coach, Jim Hurst, and a host of other wonderful teachers made for a great place of encouragement. The teachers there helped build a foundation for many additional years of learning, learning that has not stopped.

Thanks go to Brad Gaines and Chad Celi, a couple of great marketing geniuses, for their encouragement to write this book. I had talked too long about it and it was Brad and Chad's encouragement that finally convinced me almost 2 years ago to make it happen. And without a good editor, this book would never make it on the shelf. Thanks to my book editor, Amy Higgs, for not being a good editor, but being a great one! And words alone are obviously not enough. Ya gotta look good too! So thanks to Karen Alsup for doing a phenomenal job as my book designer.

If you are listening to this book on audio tape, then you have already been introduced to the voice of Lee Rutherford. Lee is a phenomenal businessman, longtime client, Christian mentor, and most importantly, a great friend. Thanks Lee!

While this book is not at all a book about getting rid of Lawyers (except maybe the inefficient ones!), I did want to add a bit of levity to what is otherwise some serious discussions. So, I added a few (okay, more than a few, about 43, one for each chapter) lawyer jokes. Thanks to Dave Ahl and his very interesting website, www.SwapMeetDave.com, which helped me with coming up with a lot of my jokes.

Finally, and certainly no disrespect to close friends and colleagues of different faiths, I want to acknowledge my Christian faith. My life may not always reflect it, but please know it is nonetheless core to anything and everything I do and am about. Thanks to some special Christian mentors in my life, Rob Lake, Gene Parr, Dr. Ted Sisk, my wife, Renee, my many friends at Immanuel Baptist Church in Lexington where Renee and I were members for over 20 years and all the friends and leadership at Highview Baptist Church in Louisville, our home church now for going on 10 years.

One of life's greatest blessings is encouragement. For that, I am greatly blessed!

Contents

Preface

OK, this book is not about getting rid of lawyers. It comprises over 40 chapters of my personal advice and recommendations on a whole host of topics, all related to estate planning. Roger Madden, my law partner, has added great value with his input, editing and, at times, just plain English advice ("Jamie, you need to rewrite this section, it makes no sense").

What I want to do is give the reader the benefit of my 30-plus years of estate planning experience. While the book is directed toward individuals looking to do some estate planning, I believe that a financial advisor wanting to be better educated, or a general practice attorney wanting to move his or her practice further into the estate planning arena will also find it useful.

I also want to help make the estate planning process more efficient. The more you are prepared, the more efficient the estate planning process will be. So, while there is a lot an estate planning attorney can do to make the process more efficient, you can do a lot on your end simply by reading, and even studying, this book.

In this book, I provide many of the same illustrations and examples that I would share with you if you were in front of me, paying my $450 hourly rate. Hopefully, the chapters that relate to your situation will help you begin to think through issues to address before you go online to start planning on your own, or ahead of your initial meeting with an attorney. I have no doubt that the information in this book will point out issues, potential planning opportunities and obstacles that will help you as you journey through this very important area called *estate planning*.

Of all the services provided by lawyers, the most common is estate planning, including wills, powers of attorney, trusts, etc. This book focuses on the entire estate planning process, the changing role of the attorney in that process, and the impact non-lawyer entities are having on reshaping the way estate planning services are offered.

The roles of estate planning attorneys are changing and will continue to change as a result of the increased availability of online legal resources, along with the continued increase in the sophistication of, and training in, the financial services industry. More and more of what only lawyers used to do is now being handled either online or by non-lawyers, such as financial advisors. This book will highlight some changes in other legal practices affected by online document services and non-lawyer initiatives.

While online document companies such as LegalZoom®, NetLaw®, Rocket Lawyer® and others are the most recent entries into the estate planning market, banks, insurance companies, brokerage firms, financial planners and a host of other non-lawyer companies have been in this space for decades.

Roger Madden and I are the co-founders of NetLaw®, a company that grew out of our online estate practice that the American Bar Association said in 2012 was the best of any in the country. This book, however, is not intended to be a promotion of NetLaw, or even online document services. The goal is simply to help make the estate planning process more efficient. One way to do that is to educate our reader, before he or she hires a lawyer.

At the end of each chapter, I pose the question "End of Lawyers?" I then give you my thoughts about whether the particular topic in that chapter will require a lawyer. If not, I suggest other options. If yes, I may still give you further input on how best to relate to your attorney to make the process more efficient. As a part of what I call the "End of Lawyers" section of each chapter, I may also answer the question: "Who should be the quarterback and control the process on these types of services?" Some might argue that it should be the financial planner, others might say a trusted investment or insurance advisor, and yet others would say it must be the attorney who prepares the legal documents. Does technology change this? In some — possibly many — cases, we think it does. This book focuses on all of these issues and others surrounding estate planning.

Jamie Hargrove

INTRODUCTION/BASICS

CHAPTER 1

The Role of Online
Document Services

What's wrong with lawyer jokes?

*Lawyers don't think they're funny
and
other people don't think they're jokes.*

The past few years have been a breakthrough for online legal document services. This has been fueled in part by an estimated $40 million-plus spent by LegalZoom® each year on sales and marketing efforts that included a campaign starring famed O.J. Simpson attorney and pitchman, Robert Shapiro.[1]

The reason LegalZoom is so well known is not because it is necessarily the best, but because it has advertised its way into the forefront of the retail consumer market. Although LegalZoom may be the most familiar name in online legal documents, there are many more.

While companies for years have sold legal documents online, LegalZoom was among a small handful that utilized current technology to include a "decision tree" in the form-building process. The process works by simply asking the consumer a series of questions that would otherwise be asked by a lawyer. Based on the answers, additional questions are posed that then lead to creation of documents specific to that consumer's needs.

Though LegalZoom has been accused of participating in the unauthorized practice of law, those challenges appear to have done nothing to slow down LegalZoom or similar companies from providing online legal document services.

A lesser-known, yet also well-funded company, is Rocket Lawyer®. Rocket Lawyer has not been in the marketplace as long, but it has grown rapidly in the past few years. It is not nearly as familiar to the average consumer because its marketing strategy has been focused on Internet advertising as opposed to traditional media like TV and radio. For the Internet-savvy consumer, Rocket Lawyer may be as well-known as LegalZoom.

Both LegalZoom and Rocket Lawyer have a similar approach to legal document automation. Both offer legal documents in 25 or more practice areas or specialties. If you want to get a divorce, declare bankruptcy, start a business and

---

1 According to LegalZoom's S-1 filing in 2011, as part of its Initial Public Offering, LegalZoom spent $42 million in 2011 on sales and marketing.

create a will, you can get all of that done in one place at one time. You will also likely be assigned a single lawyer to advise you on all of those areas at the same time.

Both LegalZoom and Rocket Lawyer have networks of attorneys who support their online product offerings. In order for the attorney network system to work, the document companies must secure attorneys who are licensed in each of the states where they offer documents. Since the companies' documents are offered in all 50 states, they would each potentially start with 50 lawyers to support their documents-only service. If the companies secured a specialist in each of their various practice areas for every state, that total could increase to as many as 1,300 lawyers.

While the legal document business could be considered cutting edge, it is in some respects a throwback to the 1950s and 1960s, when most attorneys were in general practice. Starting in the 1970s and carrying over into the present day, there are hundreds of attorney specialties and subspecialties that deal with the complexities of the current U.S. legal system. Most document-only companies, with the exception of one, operate in this new industry from a "general practice" philosophy. It is certainly reasonable for these companies to originate with a very generalized practice document service, supported by generalized attorneys.

As a co-founder of NetLaw, I initiated the development of a specialized document system focused solely on estate planning as an alternative to other, generalized legal document services. At NetLaw, you can't get a divorce, declare personal bankruptcy or download an apartment lease. Instead, you can get comprehensive services on one very specific and vital part of the law.

NetLaw's business model is also different from most online legal document services. Its main focus is not to market directly to consumers, but to use a business-to-business approach. NetLaw markets its estate planning document services to business partners, including financial institutions, healthcare companies that serve the elderly, employers and charities. Those partners market NetLaw's estate planning document system to their constituents, such as clients, customers, donors and patients.

Because NetLaw's service area is specific to estate planning, users can rest assured that its document system is always current and compliant with the law. We concentrate on the ins and outs of estate planning so that our customers don't have to.

End of Lawyers? For do-it-yourself, basic documents, yes, the end is near for lawyers. However, I believe that even the simplest estate planning circumstances often require minimal involvement from a qualified attorney. Even the most basic situations can bring about issues that only a trained lawyer can anticipate, address and, many times, resolve.

CHAPTER 2

Estate Planning at Its Core

What do you have if three lawyers
are buried up to their necks in cement?

Not enough cement.

You may have heard from your tax preparer or financial advisor, or even through the media, that everyone needs a will. From a legal standpoint, this is true. To protect your loved ones, most everyone does, in fact, need a Last Will and Testament, even if you have arranged your affairs to minimize — or attempt to eliminate — probate.

Probate is a legal process required by each state that effectively wraps up a person's affairs at death. In some states, probate has been simplified, and individuals may feel comfortable handling it themselves. In other states, probate can be more complicated and require professional legal advice to navigate the process. Even relatively small estates can be subject to probate in most states. (Probate will be covered in more detail in subsequent chapters.)

If you read a lot of the self-help books on estate planning and living trusts, you might be convinced that everyone needs a living trust as well. Does everyone need a living trust? Well, probably not. For many very small estates and other straightforward situations, a simple will is more than adequate. We will get into a complete discussion of living trusts in Chapter 4.

Beyond the need for a Last Will and Testament, there are other important documents that ***everyone*** needs to have in place. They include:

- If you have young children, you need a trust under will for such children.
- General Durable Power of Attorney
- Healthcare Surrogate Designation
- Federal HIPAA Authorization
- Living Will Declaration

Some document services or lawyers will combine one or more of the above documents. For a complete discussion of some of the issues related to trusts, see Chapters 3 and 4. For more information on healthcare-related documents and end-of-life declarations, see Chapter 7.

If an individual does not have a Last Will and Testament, he or she is leaving it up to the laws of his or her state of legal residence to determine how the estate will be distributed at his or her death. Each state has its own law regarding the requirements for being a legal resident of the state. Likewise, each state has its own laws regarding intestate succession (meaning, how a person's estate is distributed if he or she dies without a will).

Many people do not go to the trouble of creating a formal will because they learn just enough about the law to develop a basic understanding of where their assets might go at the time of their death (i.e., to their kids). The problem, however, is that those laws can change or be subject to different interpretations.

Even if an individual has a Last Will and Testament, he or she may end up dying in a state other than the one where the will was drawn up. It is the laws of the state of which you are a legal resident at the time you die that govern how your assets are distributed, and not the laws at the time the will was executed. Consequently, when you change your state of legal residence, you should complete a new will that is specific to that particular state. While most states have similar laws, it is best to have a will drawn up for the state you live in now, not the state where you previously lived. If you are using an online company to prepare your will document, it is usually easy to update your will for a different state. While discussed in greater detail later, your power of attorney, healthcare surrogate designation and living will declaration/advanced directive are also very state-specific, so when you update your will for your new state of legal residence, make sure you update those documents, too.

A Last Will and Testament takes effect **only** at the time of death. It does not hold any authority over a person's affairs during his or her lifetime. Naming your brother as executor in your will does not have any impact on what happens to you should you become impaired. A general power of attorney document is most often used to appoint someone to handle your affairs when you become disabled. Someone is generally considered disabled for purposes of the power of attorney when he or she is not able to make his or her own financial decisions. I discuss in Chapter 6 the difference between an immediate power of attorney and a "springing" power of attorney. A general power of attorney document usually only covers financial affairs, not healthcare decisions. Some attorneys and online document systems, however, will combine a general power of attorney with a Healthcare Surrogate Designation.

End of Lawyers? In this case, yes. Do-it-yourself form systems are bringing about the end of lawyers in many instances. One can argue, however, that these online form systems are simply reaching individuals who would not otherwise go to an attorney. If that is true, then maybe lawyers as we know them will stick around. At least for awhile! What I think will change, however, is how attorneys gain new clients. A legal forms company can efficiently connect those consumers who really need legal representation to a trained lawyer. This dual approach of offering both a self-help process for consumers who have basic needs with an efficient process of connecting more complex cases to trained attorneys is central to companies like NetLaw. So, no, the lawyer is not going away, but he will only be used when and where he is really needed, and in a more efficient way.

TRUSTS IN GENERAL, LIVING TRUSTS AND PROBATE AVOIDANCE

CHAPTER 3

Trusts, Trusts, Trusts

How many lawyer jokes are there?

Only three.
The rest are true stories.

First on the list of necessary estate planning documents is a will. Second would be the use of a trust for your children. Why do you need a trust? Well, in over 30 years of doing tax and estate planning, I have never had a client who was comfortable with his or her estate potentially passing to an 18-year-old. In every state, a child's inheritance must be handed over to him or her upon turning age 18 if there is no trust in place. One thing a trust can do, therefore, is delay the age at which the child takes over management of, or gains unfettered control over, his or her assets.

Even if your kids are older and relatively mature, do you want your recent college graduate receiving his or her inheritance outright? While some parents might be more comfortable with a 22-year-old receiving his or her inheritance outright versus an 18-year-old, most still would prefer to protect their kids (or grandkids) by keeping the inheritance in trust until the child or grandchild is older.

One common provision is to have a spaced distribution of a beneficiary's inheritance, such as 50% at age 25 and the balance at age 30. Other clients like the idea of stretching it out a bit further, and may provide one-third at age 25, half of the balance at age 30 and the remainder at age 35. Most trusts of this type will still allow the trust funds to be used to provide for education expenses, healthcare expenses and possibly even support and maintenance.

The terms "support and maintenance" are often used in trusts. These terms refer to the basic living expenses of a trust beneficiary. Examples of support and maintenance expenses may include:

- Housing (rent or mortgage) expenses
- Automobile expenses
- Food and clothing expenses
- Insurance expenses

- Household expenses (i.e., utilities, home maintenance, etc.)

OK, let's take a step back now and talk about what a trust is and how it works. "Trust" is a very general term, just like the word "house" defines a very broad category of structures. There are brick houses, stucco houses, frame houses and on and on. So when you say, "I have a house," people know generally what you mean, but that term doesn't in any way define the look, type or purpose of the house.

The term "trust" is no different. For those who deal with trusts all the time, we know generally what that means, but we have no clue as to what that trust might be doing, its look, type or use. The trust could cover a single day, or it could be a perpetual (never-ending) trust. It could benefit my kids, or it might be used to help me avoid paying state income taxes on the sale of my business. There are just about as many forms, shapes and sizes of trusts as there are types of houses.

A trust can be created by a single, simple paragraph, like the following:

> *I, Jamie Hargrove, hereby set up this trust. I appoint myself as the trustee. The name of this trust will be the "Jamie Hargrove Really Simple Family Trust." The trustee is to hold the trust property (possibly a bank account titled in the name of the trust) for five years. The trust will then terminate and pay all of the trust assets (again, this might just be a bank account that was opened in the name of the trust with my Social Security number as the tax ID) to my lovely daughter, Lily Hargrove.*
>
> Signed: *Jamie Hargrove*
> *Settlor and Trustee*
>
> *Dated: 12/23/2014*

So, there you have it. A very simple trust. In most states, the above verbiage would meet the minimum requirements for a trust as long as the trust was "funded." To fund my trust, I simply need to go down to my bank (or to my broker/investment advisor) and open an account in the name of the trust, and put some money into the new account. Some states require the trust document be notarized and/or witnessed. Some do not.

As you can see, a trust shouldn't be anything scary and difficult. I have drafted many trusts, however, that were more than 50 pages long. Of course, I can charge more for a 50-page trust than I can for a one-paragraph trust. Just kidding!! Seriously though, it does stand to reason that a very complicated and lengthy trust will be more costly than a short and simple one. That is why, if you ask an attorney to give a general cost estimate for creating a trust, he or she is not quick to answer — because it all "depends." Do you need something short and sweet, or is your situation one that will require a lot more thought, time and attention in order to address all of the issues related to your circumstances?

The idea behind a trust in most cases is to distinctly provide for how certain assets are managed and how these assets will benefit the trust's beneficiaries. As I mentioned earlier, if I leave assets in my estate directly to my daughter, Lily, and not in trust, when she turns age 18, she has full control of those assets. Lily is the most responsible kid in the world. (Really, she is!) However, my kids — and I have four — tend to get married young. (By the way, my next book is "Marrying Young, A Guide For Parents of Kids Getting Married at a Young Age," look for it on Amazon.com soon!!)

OK, back to Lily. Even very responsible, bright kids sometimes can make really bad decisions in choosing friends, particularly whom they date or eventually marry. I had a client once who had the most beautiful, well-educated, successful and delightful daughter you would ever want to meet. Yet, I think at least half of the guys she dated or lived with had served time in jail or are serving time now. Go figure!

So what does a trust do? It is going to protect Lily from potential bad decisions or from life events that she can't even control. It is also going to protect her inheritance from claims filed by others, such as if another driver wants to sue her because of an accident the person claims was caused by Lily texting and driving. Drinking and driving used to be the biggest concern that would subject our assets to lawsuits. The magnitude of this new issue of texting and driving is really very scary. So, can a trust be designed to protect Lily's assets from that kind of a risk? Absolutely!

Did I mention that Lily's trust will protect her inheritance from the claims of her future husband? I pray that someday I'll be able to say, "I love my son-in-law." But even if that is the case, I don't want to leave my son-in-law part of Lily's inheritance. I don't care how wonderful he is and how well he treats Lily; he can take care of himself. Although the occasional client chooses otherwise, I personally want my estate to eventually pass only to my kids and future grandkids, not to my sons- or daughters-in-law.

By the way, my thinking on this issue is almost universal. If you feel guilty for thinking the same way about your children's spouses, rest assured that you are not alone. In fact, in over 30 years of practice, I can count on one hand the number of clients who thought differently.

Finally, wouldn't it be nice to know that when Lily dies, any remaining inheritance she received from her mother and me can, with certain limits, be passed on to her children free of any inheritance or estate taxes? Yes, that's right. Who knows what the estate and inheritance tax laws will be when my children die. With the trusts that I've set up for my kids, it won't matter. A significant portion, if not all, of the assets that remain will pass to my grandchildren free of any estate and inheritance taxes.

Many of my clients are concerned about a trust being too rigid or inflexible. You can certainly create a very rigid trust. You don't have to do so, however, to still provide some or all of the protections I mention in this chapter.

For example, I may put default provisions in a trust that provide for continuing trusts for my grandchildren. However, I can also provide that my kids can "reshuffle the deck" and change how the assets in the trust eventually pass on to their children or their grandchildren. The kids can have complete flexibility as to how the assets will pass on to the future generations without chipping away at any of the protections mentioned above.

Most of the trusts that I set up for my clients provide that the kids can deplete the trust if their needs so dictate. Therefore, if I know the kids are responsible, my trust planning is not a means for "controlling from the grave" but simply to give them a very flexible way to have their inheritance protected, and hence to give them even greater financial security.

I would like to end this discussion about trusts with one word: "control." A trust, quite simply, can give control or take it away. If it takes control away, let's say from a wayward child who struggles with drug abuse, the issue becomes, "Who is going to control the trust?" In all cases, I encourage my clients to consider building in advisory committees that can be a trigger for removing and/or appointing trustees of a trust. I like to use self-perpetuating committees so my advisory committee will always exist and oversee who (or which entity) is serving as trustee. I often name a three-person committee that can remove a trustee by majority vote. Also, it is "self-perpetuating," in that if one member dies, resigns or is otherwise unable to serve, the other two members will be charged with replacing the missing committee member. In other words, the committee "self-appoints" its own successors. Hence the term, "self-perpetuating."

Should I have an individual serve as trustee, or should I name a bank or trust instead? While more than half of the trusts

I have created over the years appointed individuals as their trustees, my preference is to name a bank or trust company, with the oversight of an advisory committee to "keep the institution honest." What does that mean? Are there a bunch of unscrupulous banks and trust companies out there? No, not at all. But, if you want to make sure you have the best fee arrangements and are getting the best service, I think the advisory committee needs the freedom to boot the bank or trust company out as trustee at any time. You can fire your lawyer any time, so why shouldn't you be able to fire your bank or trust company as trustee? A bank or trust company needs to know its job is on the line every day of its service as a trustee.

Why go with a bank or trust company? Because banks and trust companies are in the very business to serve as trustees. They have the systems and processes in place to serve in that capacity. They know what to do and when to do it. If you name your brother as trustee and ask him to allow your kids to pull benefits from the trust for their "health, education, support and maintenance," will your brother understand what that means? Does support and maintenance include a car? Any kind of car? How about vacations? Does he need to take into account the other resources of the kid or kids before granting their requests? A bank or trust company deals with these issues every day. Another example: Is your brother an expert in dealing with the Principal and Income Act of your particular state? Probably not. Again, a bank or trust company will know what that act is and how to interpret it.

Also, when an individual is named as a trustee in a trust, the requirement of "surety" is often waived. What that means is that the services of the individual serving as a trustee will not be covered by insurance. If the individual trustee runs off with the funds (e.g., he develops a gambling problem and "borrows" from your trust, with the intention to pay it back next week, but next week never comes), your beneficiaries (i.e., your children or other loved ones) may not have anyone to sue to get the trust money back. Of course, they could sue the trustee, but if he has lost or spent the money, good luck. With a bank or trust company, its assets stand behind the trust to make sure if there is a bad actor (even bank employees can be criminal at times), the bank or trust company will use its assets or insurance to guarantee there is no loss to the first beneficiary.

The biggest argument, however, for not using a friend or family member as a trustee is simply time. Ask yourself, "Will my brother/sister/cousin/aunt have extra time to deal with this?" I don't know about you, but if I were to ask nearly any of my friends and family if they have spare time, they would all say something like, "Are you crazy, what's that?"

If your trust is not sizeable enough to afford a bank or trust company's fees for serving as trustee, ask if they "bundle" their asset management fees with their trust administration fees. In many cases, I find that banks and trust companies may effectively give away their trust services simply to earn your asset management business. Generally, you have to pay someone to manage those assets, so why not use that leverage to negotiate lower, or possibly no-cost, trustee services?

End of Lawyers? Maybe, but probably not. I believe that when a trust of any type is determined to be the best estate planning solution, it should always be drafted or overseen by an experienced attorney. While many of the do-it-yourself legal document services provide trust forms, there is a lot more to the process than simply filling in blanks.

CHAPTER 4

Avoiding Probate: The Living Trust

Did you hear about the lawyer
hurt in an accident?

An ambulance stopped suddenly.

Chapter 3 focused on defining trusts and, particularly, trusts as an asset-protection tool for your kids, grandkids and others. This chapter will examine living trusts, which are a bit different.

For a significant portion of my practice, I was hesitant to recommend a living trust simply to avoid probate. For most of my practice, I have believed the living trust is essential when tax planning is involved. But in smaller and simpler estates, I have generally felt that a living trust may be overkill.

My attitude has changed in recent years as I have seen some of the problems caused in an electronic age that can be alleviated with a living trust plan. So, while I continue to be leery of people who say, "Everyone needs a living trust," I am advocating for living trusts more today than in the past. Because of the impact of the widespread use of online accounts, password-protected logins and other technology-related uses, having a tool that eliminates the automatic shut-off of access to one's accounts is now becoming more of a necessity.

So what is a living trust? The term itself is not a defined legal term. It generally means a trust that is established during your lifetime, as opposed to a trust that is established pursuant to your Last Will and Testament at the time of your death. Technically, therefore, a living trust could be revocable (one that can be changed or amended) or irrevocable (one that cannot be changed), such as an irrevocable life insurance trust. Over the last decade, however, the term has generally been a reference to a living "revocable" trust. Irrevocable trusts generally are not thrown into the category of "living trusts."

Some books on living trusts refer to them as a replacement for a Last Will and Testament. In most states, however, you continue to need a Last Will and Testament even if you have a living trust. Wills that are used in conjunction with a living trust are often referred to as "pour-over" wills. That is because at the time of your death most, if not all, of your assets and your estate covered in your Last Will and Testament will "pour over" into your living trust during, or upon the conclusion of, the settlement of your estate.

Those who advocate a living trust as a complete replacement for a will often argue that if a living trust is fully funded with your assets during your lifetime, there will not be any assets in your estate that are subject to your will. The problem with that assumption is that any number of circumstances could create assets in your estate, even when all of your accounts have been properly retitled in the name of your living trust. Some of those examples are:

- A tax refund. If you get a tax refund, it will not be payable to your living trust, it will be payable to you or, since you are not living, to your estate.

- Your death came as a result of someone else's negligence. Claims that your estate may have against the negligent individual may create payments to your estate.

- You simply forgot something. You have gold coins in your lockbox, and you forgot to tell your attorney about them. Or maybe you informed your attorney, but he/she never followed up with the appropriate documentation to transfer ownership into your living trust.

If any of the above occur, those items become an asset of your estate subject to your Last Will and Testament. If you have no Last Will and Testament, such assets then pass by intestate[2] succession according to state laws.

Clients often ask how a living trust avoids probate. When

---

2 Intestate is the term for when someone dies without a will. In that situation, you look to state statute as to who has rights to your assets. Generally, a spouse has certain rights, and children have certain rights. If you do not have a spouse and/or children, then parents, siblings or extended family members will have certain rights.

you die, the assets owned by you individually or titled in your name become subject to the jurisdiction of the local probate court where you died. Effectively, those individually owned assets are "probate assets." If those same assets are not in your name at death but instead are titled in the name of your living trust, such assets (again, because they are not titled in your name) are not "probate assets."

Several factors trigger the need for a living trust. They include:

- **Out-of-state real estate**: If you live in one state and own real estate in another (even a timeshare), you should give serious consideration to a living trust. Real estate is the only asset that you can own in another state that actually pulls you into that particular state's probate process. Simply having a bank account or a brokerage account in another state does not.

  If you own real estate in another state when you die, your family will be required to open up what generally is referred to as "ancillary administration." Ancillary means that it is not your primary or main probate, but an "add-on." The main probate is handled in the state in which you were a resident at your death.

  If you get pulled into another state's probate court, that often means that you have a second set of attorneys involved. Your local attorney probably will not be licensed to practice by that state's bar association. This will prompt your local attorney to engage the services of an attorney in the state in which your real estate is located. Obviously that adds time, complexity and cost to the settlement of your estate. All of that can be avoided if your out-of-state property is held (titled) in your living trust.

In order for the trust to hold title to your real estate, you must execute a deed that transfers the property from your name, or yours and your spouse's names, to the trust. The deed is then filed in the same manner it would be filed if you were selling your property to a third party. In most states, the transfer is exempt for tax purposes. Having a mortgage on the property may create some complications. You should always check with an attorney in the state where the real estate is located prior to making any transfers. If there are any consequences to the transfer in that particular state, you certainly want to know that before you make it.

- **Privacy**: Unless you are famous, mega-wealthy, or live in a very small community, privacy is probably not going to be a critical issue for you. I grew up in a very small community, Milton, Kentucky. It has a total population of around 650 people. If I still lived in Milton and had children who were living in or around there, I would have a living trust simply to keep my affairs private. In a small community, the public record aspect of the probate process can quickly become the talk of the town. In larger cities, this generally is not a factor. If, on the other hand, you are a very wealthy individual or you are a well-known public figure, the privacy aspect of a living trust is probably significant even if you are living in a larger city.

- **Streamline administration**: This is the one aspect of living trusts that is oversold. Most states have taken significant steps to simplify the probate process. Having a living trust is not going to streamline the administration of your estate any more than going to probate court and filing paperwork will. In most states, that paperwork is required whether you have assets that are in probate or not. However, to the extent that you have a living trust and have properly retitled your assets prior to your death, you can further simplify the probate of your estate.

- **Banking**: My wife handles all of our home finances. She does all of our banking online and pays many of our bills electronically with automatic payment accounts. Should she predecease me, I am in trouble! First off, the bank is going to be required to close her account. I will not be able to simply transfer that account over to my name. All of the utility bills and other bills that are being paid out of that account have to be redirected. Guess what? I don't have all of her passwords for those accounts. We've seen a lot of situations where a surviving spouse will close the account and not even think about all of the automatic bill payments coming out of it. Sometimes, the person doesn't realize it until he or she gets notice that the gas or electric is about to be shut off. If you have your bank accounts in your living trust, your death will not trigger a need for closing those accounts. Hence, your automatic payments and everything else related to your banking will continue to operate seamlessly. For many, this is becoming one of the most important reasons for a living trust.

A living trust might also be a better planning tool than a general durable power of attorney. This can be particularly true if you own a family business. If you don't have a family business, and your financial and personal affairs are fairly simple and straightforward, then having a living trust for disability planning is not important as long as you have a solid power of attorney document in place.

End of Lawyers? Maybe. Some online systems are more comprehensive than others, but certain elements still may require the assistance of a trained attorney. The titling of assets, discussed in the next chapter, becomes a critical component in the effectiveness of a living trust. More and more, however, financial advisors are equipped to advise on these issues.

CHAPTER 5

Avoiding Probate: Titling of Assets and Beneficiary Designations

What's the difference between a good lawyer and a great lawyer?

A good lawyer knows the law.
A great lawyer knows the judge.

While a living trust is an excellent tool for avoiding probate of assets titled in the trust, another way to avoid probate is via beneficiary designations; transfer on death (TOD) or payable on death (POD) designations; and possibly joint ownership with rights of survivorship or by ownership as "tenants by the entireties" (available for spouses in certain jurisdictions and similar to joint ownership with rights of survivorship).

The interaction between the way assets are titled or payable upon your death in your Last Will and Testament and/or living trust can be tricky and often confusing. It is important to understand what controls how assets are transferred at your death. Here are some examples of how assets can transfer outside of probate without the use of a living trust:

- Where assets are owned jointly "with survivorship" or where assets are owned by married persons as "tenants by the entirety:"

  - **Real estate** (residence, investment property, etc.), if owned by two individuals (e.g., husband and wife), will pass automatically to the survivor at the first co-owner's death if the property was titled in their joint names "with right of survivorship" or if it was owned by spouses as "tenants by the entirety."

    Most attorneys, when asked to put the home in the joint names of a husband and wife, will almost always title it with "survivorship." Because the "survivorship" nature of the deed dictates the transfer of the deceased owner's interest in the property to the survivor(s), the property is not subject to the probate process.

  - **Joint bank or investment accounts** can also be titled "jointly with survivorship" or owned by spouses as "tenants by the entirety" and, if so, the deceased owner's interest in the account will automatically pass to the surviving account holder or holders. In that case, the account is not subject to the probate process.

- Where an asset or account's ownership, at the account holder's death, is directed via a beneficiary designation, a "payable on death (POD)" or a "transfer on death (TOD)" designation:

  – **Life insurance** proceeds payable via a beneficiary designation are not subject to probate as long as they are not payable to the insured's estate or executor, since the proceeds will be paid directly to the beneficiary.

  – **Retirement plans** (401(k), profit-sharing, IRA, etc.) payable via a beneficiary designation are not subject to probate as long as the plans' proceeds are not payable to the deceased account holder's estate or executor, since the proceeds will be paid directly to the designated beneficiary.

  – **Bank or brokerage accounts** with "POD" or "TOD" designations will not be subject to probate, since the account's ownership or assets will pass directly to the person designated.

- Where an asset has been transferred with a retained interest[3], the retained interest will pass at death outside of probate and without regard to the terms of a will or living trust:

  – **Life estates** are not routine, but can serve as an effective transfer for a parcel of real estate. A life estate results when you transfer a "remainder

---

3 A retained interest is created when an asset (i.e., real estate) or an interest in a trust is transferred to someone with the person making the transfer retaining some type of economic interest in the transferred asset.

interest" in property while reserving the right during your lifetime to use the property. This retained right is called a "reservation of a life estate interest" in the property. Upon your death, the property then passes to the "remainderman," who may be your children or other individuals or trusts. The passing of full title in the property to the remainderman occurs outside of probate. For example, a widowed father might transfer his residence to his only child and retain a life estate. He would be able to reside in the house until his death and then, immediately at the father's death, his child would be able to freely use or dispose of the property.

- **Split-interest trusts** are trusts that allow for reservation of an interest in the assets being transferred to a particular type of trust. Examples of such trusts are charitable remainder trusts and grantor retained annuity trusts. In each case, assets are transferred to a trust, and the person making the transfer retains an interest in either the income or other rights in the assets held in such trust. Upon such person's death or the expiration of a period of time, ownership passes to a remainderman outside of probate.

As referenced above, the way assets are titled (or the way beneficiary designations are drafted/completed) impacts whether those assets will be subject to the probate process or, alternatively, pass outside of probate. The bigger issue, however, is making sure those assets impacted by their titling (or beneficiary designation) end up where you want them to go. In other words, did the person you wanted to benefit from that particular asset actually end up with the asset?

People diligently execute their Last Will and Testaments, but when they eventually die, their loved ones often find that the otherwise well-designed Last Will and Testament had little to do with distribution of assets. Let me give you an example.

Assume that Bob and Jane are in their 60s and have been married for 10 years. They each have kids from previous marriages. Bob sets up his will to provide that one-third of his estate goes to his kids and two-thirds goes to Jane, his second wife. But then Bob dies, and none of his assets pass to his kids. Why?

Bob's assets were as follows:

- Joint checking account with Jane
- Joint savings account with Jane
- CD titled in both his and Jane's names with "or"
- A life insurance policy with a beneficiary designation naming Jane
- A small government pension fund with a beneficiary designation naming Jane
- An IRA with a beneficiary designation naming Jane
- A personal residence that was purchased after he and Jane got married and was put in both names (Bob and Jane) as "joint tenants with right of survivorship"
- A new Toyota Avalon in only Bob's name

In Bob's will, he had a provision that left his "personal property" to his wife, which included all of his jewelry, collectables, household furnishings and his new Toyota Avalon. The "rest and residue" of his estate (everything else, including stocks, bonds, real estate, etc.) was to pass one-third to his kids and two-thirds to his wife. The problem, however, was that the way he titled all of his assets (other than the tangible personal property) left nothing subject to the provisions of his will.

The good news is that all of Bob's assets (except the Avalon) passed free of probate to Jane. The bad news (at least for Bob's kids) is that despite what appeared to be a clear intent to leave them a significant portion of his estate (i.e., one-third), the way in which he titled his assets left everything to Jane, his second wife.

So, for example, Bob's personal residence was held with his wife in "survivorship," which means at his death, ownership automatically passed to his wife. All of the joint bank accounts were set up as "survivorship," so again, at his death, all of those accounts passed to his wife and were not in any way subject to his will. It should be noted that Bob never really understood what the impact of a joint account with his wife was. While a joint account need not necessarily be set up as a survivorship account, most bankers will use the survivorship designation as the default for how to title an account between spouses.

Finally, Bob's life insurance, pension, 401(k) and IRA plans were all set up with beneficiary designations that left them to his wife, with his kids as secondary beneficiaries. None of these accounts are controlled by his Last Will and Testament.

As you can see, a will, living trust and related documents are only valuable in terms of asset distribution at death if assets are appropriately titled.

If you have a living trust, you want to pay special attention to titling your assets in such a way that they actually end up owned by, or payable to, your living trust. If you want to avoid probate, you must transfer your assets to the living trust during your lifetime and/or have the relevant accounts or insurance policies made payable to the trust or intended recipient (just not your estate).

How assets are titled can impact who pays the inheritance and/or estate tax, if any. Let's assume, in the Bob and Jane example, that Bob had assets of $150,000 in his own name. Also assume that Bob and Jane were not legally married but were living together for 10 years. Some fairly significant state inheritance taxes will be due in many states. It would not be uncommon for the tax rate to be as much as 16%, if not more, for assets passing to Jane. If Jane has more than $1 million coming to her via 401(k)s, IRAs, etc., it could trigger an inheritance tax that would more than eat up the $150,000 of assets that were in Bob's name, at least $50,000 of which were intended for his children. In this scenario, Bob's entire probate estate of $150,000 will be used to pay the inheritance taxes. In other words, the kids end up bearing Jane's tax on assets that were intended to come to them. The "fix" to a problem like this is to make sure the Last Will and Testament or living trust clearly directs how taxes are to be handled. This is an example of an estate in which customization of the "tax payment clause" in the will or trust is needed to ensure that the taxes are offset against the correct beneficiaries.

Beneficiary designations and how your assets are titled not only affects whether those assets pass through probate or free of probate, but they can also impact the ultimate beneficiary of such assets. Such titling can also impact tax-payment clauses in a will or living trust.

End of Lawyers? Maybe. You do not have to be a lawyer to advise individuals on how to title their assets for the purposes of their estates and financial plans. Experienced financial advisors and accountants can provide guidance in this important area. More often, however, an attorney will have more complete knowledge and experience with deed transfers or other retitling procedures. As financial advisors and accountants continue to offer broader services, they certainly may be equipped to assist with asset titling and retitling, leaving only deeds for attorneys to prepare.

POWER OF ATTORNEY AND HEALTHCARE DOCUMENTS

CHAPTER 6

General Durable Power of Attorney

What do you call 25 skydiving lawyers?

Skeet.

In an earlier chapter, I addressed the argument that everyone does not need a Last Will and Testament. OK, that may be true for some individuals. But I, along with the majority of attorneys, believe that everyone does need a general durable power of attorney. This document lets you name someone to manage your financial affairs if you are unable to do so. You may believe that the state laws or the way you title your accounts will be sufficient to handle your estate and financial situation upon your death. Should you become incapacitated, however, there is no substitute for a general durable power of attorney. Someone you trust needs to have the legal authority to make decisions should you have a stroke, car accident or other circumstance that renders you unable to make your own financial decisions.

Without a general durable power of attorney, the process to appoint someone to make your financial decisions is very involved, and it can be costly in some circumstances. In some states, it ultimately involves a jury trial that will declare your incompetency to make financial decisions and appoint a guardian, conservator or committee to make those decisions for you. In most states, it is not an expensive process because it is often controlled and monitored by the court system itself. However, it is very time-consuming and involves a process that most people would not want their loved ones to endure. There will be a required psychiatric evaluation and other medical assessments, which are then submitted to the court to document your incapacity.

A general durable power of attorney can either be a "springing" power or one that takes effect immediately upon signing, sometimes called an "immediate" power.

A "springing" power becomes effective only upon the occurrence of certain events or conditions. Some of my clients like the idea of not naming someone who will immediately have very broad powers to control or otherwise direct their financial affairs. The fact that such document takes effect only upon their disability can be comforting.

My personal philosophy is that if you don't trust someone enough to name them immediately while you are competent and have the ability to revoke such power, then you shouldn't name that individual as your representative when you become incapacitated. The reason I like an immediate power versus a springing power of attorney is that with a springing power, you have to define potential future conditions or disabilities. The problem lies in how you define those terms and what procedures or documentation will be required to prove that you have, in fact, become disabled or incapacitated.

The next problem is the people, particularly financial institutions, who need to rely upon the springing power of attorney. If the conditions have not been met, the document is worthless, and no one will be authorized to act on your behalf. If these institutions allow someone to act on your behalf, they have potential liability. Because of that, financial institutions are very cautious about accepting springing powers of attorney. The process involves sending the document to their legal department to review and give an opinion as to whether the conditions have been met and are sufficient to recognize the appointed power of attorney designee. With an immediate power of attorney, you won't run into these potential roadblocks.

A general durable power of attorney is revocable and thus allows you to name someone today whom you trust. If, for any reason, that person becomes a concern, you can immediately revoke the power of attorney.

Similar issues can arise with how you name successor individuals to serve as your backup power of attorney. If you or your loved one is elderly, you may want to consider naming joint attorneys-in-fact, rather than a succession listing. So instead of naming your spouse and then one or more of your children, you may want to simply name your spouse **and** one or more of your children, with each able to act independently.

Assume that your father is 78 years old and your mother is 75. They are both in relatively good health. They would likely designate each other as their attorney-in-fact and then name one or more of their children as a successor. The challenge in this very common situation lies in determining whether the spouse is no longer able to serve as a power of attorney. If there is a succession designation, generally the successor only has powers upon the death or disability of the earlier-named appointee.

Let's assume that your father is incapacitated, and while your elderly mother may not technically be incapacitated, she clearly is not in a position to handle their finances. She can sign a document waiving her right to serve, but the question remains whether she has capacity to enter into that document. A financial institution examining that document will be concerned about whether the conditions for the successor to be empowered have been met. Just as with a springing power, you find yourself in a situation where a financial institution may have to assess whether they feel comfortable about recognizing the backup or successor attorney-in-fact. Leaving this determination in the hands of financial institutions can cause a lot of headaches.

An easy solution is to name several people who may act either jointly or individually. If this is a situation with a high level of trust among all family members, this group designation approach is recommended. That way, if any one person becomes incapacitated or dies, the others may continue to act on your behalf.

End of Lawyers? Probably. In many situations, a lawyer is not necessary to execute a general durable power of attorney. While complexities can develop, usually they are triggered not by issues related to the general power of attorney drafting process itself, but from other, unrelated issues, such as second marriages or situations where family conflict arises.

Jamie Hargrove

CHAPTER 7

Healthcare Planning

What do you throw to a drowning lawyer?

His partners.

When it comes to healthcare issues and estate planning, there are generally three principal documents that need to be considered. While everyone needs these three basic documents, the people with the greatest need for them are the elderly and young adults.

As you get older, the risk of impairment or disability that could render you unable to make your own healthcare decisions significantly increases. If Grandma suddenly has a stroke and does not have the proper legal documents in place, who will make decisions regarding her treatment?

Another group that has a great need for healthcare documents are college-age youth. Once your child turns age 18, that child is technically an adult, and you no longer have the legal authority to make your son or daughter's healthcare decisions. If your daughter is in college halfway across the country and becomes injured and unconscious, who will make decisions about her care? How are you going to obtain information and updates on her condition from her doctors and other healthcare providers? In most states, as well as under federal law, you as a parent are not automatically given authority over the healthcare decisions of an adult child. That adult child, therefore, needs to give you that decisional responsibility in the form of a legal document immediately upon turning age 18.

Once that child gets married, the decision-maker is likely to become his or her spouse. Until that time, however, your children are most likely going to want you to have the authority to make their very important healthcare decisions.

Healthcare Surrogate Designation: Just as a general power of attorney gives you the authority to make your financial decisions (either immediately or when you become incapacitated), a healthcare surrogate designation gives a trusted family member or friend similar authority for making healthcare decisions.

A healthcare surrogate designation authorizes one or more people to make decisions relative to which type of treatment you should receive, the location of that treatment and who will deliver such treatment.

Do you name one person and a successor, or do you simply name a group of people? As a general rule, I do not advise naming a group if all of them must agree. If you want to name multiple people, consider allowing any one of the named individuals to make decisions. If your children or the relevant group of appointees are on good terms with each other, and you fully expect them to reach consensus concerning your healthcare, then naming all of your children (or other group of appointees) may be fine as long as you allow each one the ability to sign off individually. However, if you think your kids (or other group of appointees) will not be able to reach consensus, you should name only the one you trust most to make healthcare decisions.

In some states, your living will is combined with a healthcare surrogate designation. In most of those cases, however, the healthcare surrogate designation only applies to end-of-life decisions relative to the living will declaration. In other words, the healthcare surrogate named in that document is appointed solely to make decisions relative to resuscitation and the provision of food, hydration, etc., but they are not able to make broader healthcare decisions. If you have such a document but do not also include a broader healthcare surrogate designation, you need to supplement that document with a distinct designation.

Some attorneys like the idea of combining a healthcare surrogate designation and a general durable power of attorney. I like to keep those documents separate. Some individuals who do not have the time or capability to serve as your attorney-in-fact under the general power of attorney may be most able, and willing, to serve as your healthcare surrogate. Resigning from one and not the other when they are combined in the same document can get a bit confusing. If the documents are separate, it is very easy to resign or decline one role but remain in power in the other.

HIPAA Authorization: While a healthcare surrogate designation appoints a person to make your healthcare decisions, a HIPAA authorization grants access to your healthcare information. Your healthcare surrogate designation comes under the authority of state law, but a HIPAA authorization is a healthcare document prescribed by the federal government under the Health Insurance Portability and Accountability Act (commonly referred to as HIPAA). As such, healthcare surrogates are not given access to healthcare information unless they also are authorized pursuant to a HIPAA authorization. As a general rule, you'll name the same individuals for your HIPAA authorization as you have in your healthcare surrogate designation.

For your healthcare surrogate, you may decide to appoint your spouse and then name each of your children in order of preference. You may want to consider having your HIPAA authorization name the entire group rather than a priority order.

Keep in mind that a healthcare surrogate designation grants power to make a decision. A HIPAA authorization does not grant any decisional authority, but simply grants access to information.

Let me give you an example. Let's assume your husband has named you as his healthcare surrogate and your oldest child, Jane, as his backup or successor. Then assume that there has been an accident, your husband needs critical care, he cannot make his own decisions and you have to go to work. In many family situations, mom or dad may want the kids to be included in doctor's meetings and have other access to their dad's health information so they can support and counsel their parents in making the right healthcare decisions. By including the kids on the HIPAA authorization, they may participate in the decision-making process without giving any of them the authority to make the decisions.

Living Will Declaration: The living will declaration, like the healthcare surrogate designation, is a document very specific to each state's law, giving specific guidelines on end-of-life decisions. Most states now offer a statutory form, but in most states this form is not required. Many attorneys who specialize in estate planning provide their own forms that incorporate much of the information on the statutory form, but add additional provisions and directives that state statutory forms often omit.

In over 30 years of practice, an overwhelming majority of my clients have asked me to draw up a living will declaration for them. While a living will declaration can certainly say you do not want life support removed under any circumstances, that is rare. I have found that most people wish to have life support removed only when it is certain that their situation is irreversible and that there is little chance they will retain a certain quality of life.

There seems to be two extremes for living will declarations. Most attorneys use a form that follows the state statute closely and has few, if any, options relative to the declaration. On the extreme opposite end of the scale is a document called a "loving will." The process to develop loving wills is long and involved. They recognize that, in many end-of-life situations, the issues you face are often more complex than a simple yes or no as to "pulling the plug." States have not officially adopted these more extensive forms.

End of Lawyers? Maybe. As with a general power of attorney, oftentimes extenuating circumstances and family dynamics create issues that must be addressed by trained lawyers. Will an online system adequately address the delicate issues related to life support and healthcare decision making? Can it take into consideration family conflicts, blended families or second marriages? Can other advisors help in this area? Certainly they can. Working with a trained attorney to plan for the worst could make the difference in your critical time of need.

CHILDREN, THEIR INHERITANCE AND THEIR TRUSTS

CHAPTER 8

Uniform Gift to Minors Act and Uniform Transfer to Minors Act Accounts

How can you tell when a lawyer is lying?

Jamie Hargrove

His lips are moving.

Assets inherited by or given to a minor (an individual under age 18) must either be turned over to such minor's guardian or custodian or go into an account that is monitored and controlled by the guardian/custodian. In most states, a parent is not automatically legal guardian/custodian for the purposes of controlling a minor's assets.

For example, assume that a grandchild receives an outright inheritance of $100,000 from his or her grandparents. In the absence of a statute providing otherwise, one or both of the minor's parents would need to go to court to have themselves appointed as the guardian over such funds.

Fortunately, the cost and complexity of these types of guardianship proceedings for minors are avoided with relatively standard statutes passed in each state. Such statutes are generally referred to as the Uniform Gift to Minors Act (UGMA) or the Uniform Transfer to Minors Act (UTMA).

Such accounts generally provide that a gift or transfer made to a minor can be set up in an account designated under that particular state's statutes and do not require the court to appoint a specified guardian. The custodian of the account is specified by the person making the gift or transfer at the time the account is set up. This ensures the ease of transfers to minors and has become a very common practice.

Despite all this, I seldom advise the use of UGMA/UTMA accounts! The biggest problem with such accounts is that upon turning age 18, the minor has full access to the account's assets. In over 30 years of practice, I don't remember having a client who felt comfortable with his or her child or grandchild gaining access to significant assets upon turning age 18. With the influence of college, friends, potential marriage partners and other issues, giving a teen access to substantial funds could have a more detrimental than positive impact, even when the child is perceived as very responsible.

Some people incorrectly assume that an UGMA/UTMA account is going to shift taxable income from the higher income tax bracket of a parent or grandparent to the lower tax bracket (or no tax bracket) of a minor child or grandchild. Not true. When a parent sets up an UGMA/UTMA account for a child, the income on such account is still taxed back to the parent.

The questions I hear most often about UGMA/UTMA accounts are generally not related to establishing an account. Instead, they are questions about how to shift the UGMA/UTMA account into a trust or other vehicle that will allow UGMA/UTMA funds to be protected upon the minor's 18th birthday.

One scenario is where Mom, Dad or a grandparent sets up an UGMA/UTMA account, makes gifts into it over several years and creates a sizable account, only later to fear the implications of granting the minor immediate access to the funds on his or her 18th birthday.

There is not a lot that can be done, although many have tried. Think of it this way: if you had a 40-year old son with a $50,000 account, would it be reasonable for you to go to your son and tell him you are going to take his $50,000 account and tie it up in a trust or other vehicle? You would say no, that's ridiculous. Well, an UGMA/UTMA account is really no different. When a gift has been made, a gift has been made. You cannot take it back. So while it seems like there should be a difference, there really isn't.

Assuming the account exists (because if it doesn't, don't start one), the best solution is to establish a trust that is set up by the individual turning age 18. You then convince the 18-year-old to transfer his or her UGMA/UTMA account into the new trust. Of course, if the 18-year-old is already irresponsible and into all kinds of trouble, that may be problematic. If the concern, however, is what can happen between ages 18 and, say, 25, this may be a good solution. The parent or grandparent can "sweeten the deal" by agreeing to put some additional monies into such trust if the child or grandchild will agree to the trust transaction.

The terms of the trust can provide for the parent, grandparent, other individual or institution to serve as the trustee so that the funds can continue to be managed by someone other than the young person.

The terms of the trust can also provide for how the funds will eventually come back to, or otherwise benefit, the child or grandchild who established the trust in the first place. It can provide for the continued use of funds for tuition and other educational expenses. It also can provide that upon a certain age (e.g., 25, 30 or another milestone age) the trust will terminate and return the funds back to the child or grandchild who originally started with the UGMA/UTMA account.

Some people have attempted to create trusts for the UGMA/UTMA accounts prior to the child or grandchild turning age 18, with such trusts set up by the parent, guardian or grandparent. The terms of those trusts, if even allowed by a particular state, generally are going to require that, upon the minor turning age 18, the trust must terminate. At a minimum (which is usually the case in these types of trusts) the trust would simply provide notice to the 18-year-old that he or she has the ability (during a reasonable withdrawal period) to withdraw such funds from the trust. There would have to be clear notice to the individual turning age 18 and a reasonable amount of time for such individual to withdraw the funds. Sixty to 90 days is reasonable.

Most states do not have much, if any, statutory or case law authority to establish these types of trusts. As long as the funds are managed properly, there is not a whole lot of risk to try the trust approach. If it doesn't work, the worst thing that happens is the UGMA/UTMA beneficiary gains rights to the assets — which is what would have happened if you never attempted the trust planning. If it works, you may have effectively protected not only the assets but also the child or grandchild from any harm that may result from irresponsible handling of funds.

A final approach would be to consider making investments in assets that are not very liquid. For example, some of my clients establish a family limited partnership (FLP) or family limited liability company (FLLC)[4]. They contribute some of their own funds and also have the UGMA/UTMA accounts contribute into these investment entities. The UGMA/UTMA account becomes the owner of the partnership interest or the membership interest in an LLC. Those membership interests, even if voting interests, generally would not have an overall controlling interest in the LLC or partnership.

The result is that the individual beneficiary, upon turning age 18, gains access to his UGMA/UTMA assets, but such assets are now in the form of a non-liquid investment in a family partnership or a FLLC. Effectively, the young beneficiary does not have access to cash to spend or assets to liquidate.

Some states may restrict this type of maneuver. Again, the worst thing that could happen is that a child figures out the maneuver is not appropriate and seeks to have his or her FLP or FLLC membership interests liquidated. If that happens, and if it looks like you have no other legal authority, you still are not in any worse position than if you had not attempted to protect the assets.

End of Lawyers? Yes and no. Certainly, to establish an UGMA/UTMA account, a lawyer is not needed. To create a trust that will extend the time period a child or grandchild receives funds out of a UGMA/UTMA account, an attorney should be involved. An attorney should also be involved if you decide to change the form of the UGMA/UTMA investment from something very liquid to something non-liquid, like an FLP or FLLC.

---

4 A FLP and FLLC are each business entities generally established under a particular state's business statutes. Fillings to organize and maintain a FLP or FLLC are generally handled through the state's office of the Secretary of State. Most states now provide online information and allow for online filings.

CHAPTER 9

Simple Kid's Trusts vs. Lifetime Family Protection Trusts

What do you call a lawyer gone bad?

Jamie Hargrove

Senator.

I am generally surprised when I hear from wealthy people, or even those with more modest estates, who have established trusts for their children that provide for the trust assets to be distributed at certain ages and for the trust to eventually terminate. Certainly, if you have a couple hundred thousand dollar estate with no life insurance and three children, that may be OK. But in most cases, a lifetime family protection trust may be a much better option.

An example of a simple child's trust would be assets held in a single trust until the youngest child reaches a certain age, or graduates from college, and then makes distributions based on certain ages.

Two common sets of age distributions for this type of simple trusts would be:

- Half at age 25 and the balance at age 30;
- One-third at age 25, one-third of the balance at age 30 and the remaining balance at age 35.

Usually in simple children's trusts, the trusts will provide for the "health, education, support and maintenance" of a child along with receiving distributions at age 25, 30 and possibly 35. Asking clients about how to structure their children's trusts is a little bit like taking a poll. How you ask the question makes all the difference in the results of the poll.

As an example, the following question is pretty likely to result in a simple child's trust, with the trust terminating at age 30 or 35, or some other milestone age established by the client. The question is:

> "At what age do you want to ultimately distribute the assets of your children's trust to them?"

First, the question presumes that you need to come up with a set age. Many times, an attorney won't offer a lifetime family protection trust as an option. If an attorney does offer this option, it may be in the context of something like this:

> *"Do you want your trust to continue for the lifetime of your children, or do you want to simply provide that, at certain ages, the trust will be distributed to the children?"*

A high percentage of the time, my clients would focus on questions like, "At what age will my children be responsible?" Or maybe, "At what age will they be settled down?" I believe that when asked in this manner, most individuals will select the simple child's trust.

If, however, the question is asked this way:

> *"Mr. Jones, if I could create a trust for your children that protects the assets in each child's separate trust from claims made by his or her spouse (including claims from a divorce or other marital rights that may attach at the time of their death); and I could protect those assets against creditors who may sue your child or children over claims of negligent acts (e.g., drinking and driving, texting and driving, bad business deals, etc.); and I could ensure the assets that remain at each child's death, if any, would pass free of probate, free of any state inheritance taxes and free of any federal estate taxes, do you think you might be interested in that type of trust?"*

When the question is asked like this, at least in my practice, over 90% of clients want the lifetime family protection trust.

Another question I ask is:

> *"If you could provide these protections and yet give each child control and access (at the age you specify) to his or her assets, does it not make sense to allow those assets to stay in trust to continue*

those protections rather than terminating the trust at age 30 or 35 and completely losing all of those asset protection benefits for your children?"

I have some clients who set up lifetime family protection trusts for the sole purpose of giving their children the opportunity to "grow the trust" with their own business deals and investments. When investments and businesses start from inside the trust that Mom or Dad sets up, they can provide significant asset protection barriers.

I might have clients who say they would just as soon let the children have their inheritance outright, allowing the children to set up their own trusts.

Here's the problem. Once the children receive their inheritance or the distribution out of the trust, any trust they might then try to establish will be far inferior to the trust their parents could have established for them.

The trusts that parents set up for children can grant all kinds of rights, access and control. The trusts the children set up themselves, however, cannot have such retained access and control and still have all of the above protections. So if you take the approach, "I'll just leave it to the kids and let them deal with it," you are effectively eliminating an asset protection tool and plan that they cannot duplicate. Once the assets go to your children outright, they no longer have a plan that protects their assets while giving them control and access to those assets. In order for your children to have protections similar to what your trust planning could give them, the children effectively will have to give their inheritance away. That's not likely to happen.

So, if you could create a trust that gives your children, at the appropriate ages, access to their assets, the ability to control the trust, to serve as their own trustees and the flexibility to redirect the assets during lifetime or at death, why would you not want that trust?

Nowhere in my description above did I say that setting up this trust is a reaction to fears or concerns that the children are irresponsible. Even if we assume that the children will be totally responsible, does the trust still make sense? Absolutely!

While I will not receive a large inheritance, whatever inheritance I do receive will come to me via a family protection trust. I've been married for over 30 years, I'm an attorney, a CPA, and I am fiscally responsible. I appear to be a candidate for receiving my inheritance outright. However, I do not want my inheritance outright because I want it to be protected. While it might be nice if my parents set up my lifetime protection trust with the belief that I could leave it in further trust for my wife (with plenty of restrictions to make sure her next husband doesn't benefit), why wouldn't I want that trust for the protection of me, my wife and my children? In my case, I do. I truly believe that if properly explained, the majority of people would prefer to have the family protection trust.

If you decide to implement a family protection trust, one question you will want to address is whether to give each of your children the ability to leave some or all of the trust assets in further trust for their spouses, as I described above for my own trust. I tend to encourage clients to leave that flexibility to the child. If a client had a clause that terminated the trust at a certain age anyway, in that situation the child would have the ability to leave the assets for the benefit of his or her spouse with no restrictions whatsoever. So it makes sense to leave it up to the child to determine whether he or she wants to allow a spouse to benefit in any way from the assets in the trust.

When a trust includes such provisions for a spouse, I provide that the trust must be restricted, in that only an income or income-type interest is granted. In other words, the goal is to restrict the access to the principal of the trust assets but allow your son or daughter to provide an income interest to his or her spouse.

I have, on occasion, provided for a limited amount that the son or daughter can set aside for the benefit of a spouse. For example, I have used 50% as the maximum amount that can be set aside for the benefit of a husband or wife, with the balance required to pass on to the children.

End of Lawyers? No, lawyers are pretty safe when a family protection trust is utilized. For simple trusts, however, the answer may be yes. While not all online legal document services offer trusts for children, many do. My company, NetLaw, has various options — including the ones mentioned above — for use in creating simple children's trusts.

CHAPTER 10

Incentive Trusts: Make a Buck, Get a Buck

What's the difference between a lawyer and a vulture?

Jamie Hargrove

The lawyer gets frequent flyer miles.

There are many benefits to using trusts in estate planning. One such benefit is that a trust can be used as an asset protection tool. As discussed in Chapter 3, trusts are used quite often to protect assets from claims made by your children's spouses or creditors, as well as from inheritance and estate taxes.

Trusts can also be used, however, to incentivize your beneficiaries. It's simple. Put in place conditions for certain rewards. These can be virtually anything: "If you do X, then you can have Y out of the trust." I am hesitant to give too many examples in this chapter because such examples might be limiting in some people's minds. There really are no limits when it comes to incentive trusts.

Of course, the problem with any type of trust arrangement, or even outright bequest, is the negative impact it could have on a beneficiary. We all hope that it will create positive results. Unfortunately, I hear too often about family situations that tell a different story. That's where an incentive trust could play an important role.

One such trust arrangement could include a "pre-nuptial incentive clause." A trust may give broad benefits and rights to a spouse. Those rights may continue after your death and beyond a subsequent marriage. However, this is only if a valid pre-nuptial agreement exists to protect the pre-marital, non-marital assets of the trust beneficiary from marital claims of a new spouse. In this situation, the trust itself is not providing the protections per se as much as it is saying to a beneficiary: protect yourself and the trust will give you certain rights, benefits and access to its assets.

With children, the use of a pre-nuptial incentive provision is much more limited. In most jurisdictions, the trust itself will protect assets set up for the beneficiary. If the assets are in trust, and the child/beneficiary does not have any assets of his or her own, a pre-nup is not as important. Language in the trust agreement to encourage beneficiaries to enter into their own pre-nuptial agreement therefore may not be necessary because the assets (in the trust) are already protected. My advice is, "don't sweat the small stuff." Don't try to tie up every asset. It's not worth it. One asset to leave alone might be the personal residence. Many times, there can be significant issues when an in-law feels like he or she is living in someone else's house.

Another type of incentive trust provision concerns income. With an income incentive trust, the focus is to encourage a beneficiary or beneficiaries to seek and sustain a job, rather than simply live off the trust assets. Over the years, many of my clients have expressed reluctance to create trust funds for kids, grandkids or other loved ones because they don't want it to appear that they are encouraging their beneficiaries to drop out of school or simply be lazy. An income provision in the trust can discourage that scenario.

An income incentive trust is oftentimes fairly simple. The terms may be as simple as saying that for every dollar a beneficiary earns in earned income or from his or her business or employment, he or she will be entitled to a $1 match. Of course, the match can be set at any amount and can be capped as well as indexed for inflation.

An income incentive trust can also address situations where a son or daughter is not generating any of his or her own income, but not because he or she is waiting around for trust benefits. For example, assume that you have three daughters, and one of them decides she wants to be a stay-at-home mom. The other two daughters have good jobs in steady professions and are entitled to matching distributions from each of their respective trusts. To ensure that the stay-at-home mom is not cut out of her benefits, the income-match provisions can be expanded to say that, if an individual beneficiary is married, the trust may provide for a match based on the couple's income, not just the direct beneficiary. This, however, would not address a single mom who may want to stay home to care of the kids and live only off trust income.

An incentive trust would also not be the best option when one beneficiary is less financially successful than the others. For example, let's assume you have three daughters, and two become very successful in their professions. The third has decided to help the needy and down-trodden, and takes an important, but very low-paying, position with a local relief organization. Of the three, she's the hardest working, yet makes the least money. Under a strict incentive trust, she may receive the least amount in assets even though she is the one who could benefit most from the additional financial support.

In both of these examples, one way to determine whether an incentive trust provision works for all beneficiaries over the long term is to grant authority to other family members or advisors, which will allow them to adjust the incentive provisions. Such discretionary trusts are discussed in Chapter 11. I might also advise clients to create a fixed-benefit trust and add in the discretionary powers of a committee, which would allow for changes to some of the terms in the trust. "Discretionary" simply means giving decision-making powers, or "discretion," to an individual, committee or trustee. A fixed-interest trust is also discussed in detail in Chapter 11.

End of Lawyers? No. Lawyers will continue to be in demand in this area of estate planning. To ensure that all beneficiaries are treated equally under the provisions of a trust, a trained attorney should be involved. The complexities of incentive clauses call for legal experience that most consumers or online legal forms services cannot provide.

CHAPTER 11

Discretionary Trust vs. Fixed-Interest Trust

An Observation by Sandra Day O'Connor

"There is no shortage of lawyers in Washington, DC."

"In fact, there may be more lawyers than people."

When establishing a trust for the benefit of your children or other beneficiaries, you have to determine what rights or benefits you want to give them. There really are no absolutes when it comes to how you want a beneficiary to benefit from a trust. You can be as creative as you want and provide all kinds of "if this, then that" provisions. Or you can establish a simple trust that provides for all of the income to be paid out and the principal (or "corpus") to be used for the "health, education, support and maintenance" needs of the beneficiary.

When thinking about the beneficiary's trust distribution rights, you should think in terms of income and principal. Income, as you might imagine, is the money that the trust's assets earn each year. Income generally includes such things as interest and dividends. Capital gains, however, are generally not treated as income.

Let me give you an example. Assume you set up a trust and put $100,000 in it. At the end of the first year, it earns 4% interest and dividend income, for a total of $4,000. At the end of the year, therefore, you have principal of $100,000 and income of $4,000. Most trusts will separate rights to income and rights to principal into different provisions. This is primarily done for tax purposes, but there are other reasons for making the distinction between income and principal.

Continuing the above example, assume that the $100,000 was, in part, invested in Apple® stock. There was a $10,000 investment made in Apple stock that was sold at the end of the first year for $12,000. Now, we have $4,000 in interest and dividend income and $2,000 of capital gains ($12,000 less $10,000). The capital gains amount is generally not going to be treated as income. It will simply be added to the principal so that, at the end of the year, you have principal assets of $102,000 and income of $4,000.

Here are some examples of income distribution provisions:

1. Payment of all income;
2. Payment of all income for "health, education, support and maintenance" needs;
3. Payment of income at the discretion of the trustee.

The first two items above are fixed-interest provisions. The first one is easily recognized as a fixed-interest provision, in that no discretion whatsoever is exercised by the trustee or anyone else. Whatever income is generated by the trust is paid out to the beneficiary. No one has to think about whether the requirements of the trust have been met by the beneficiary. Income is generated. Income is paid out.

In the second provision, there is some degree of discretion. It must be determined whether the beneficiary's needs are consistent with the terms of "health, education, support and maintenance." Many times, the provisions in a trust may actually say something along the lines of: "The trustee, at the trustee's discretion, shall pay income to the beneficiary for the beneficiary's health, education, support and maintenance" needs.

While there is some degree of discretion required by the trustee in the above example, the reality is that, in most states, once you use the terms "health, education, support and maintenance," you have given defined rights to the beneficiary. So, for example, let's assume a beneficiary wanted to have his reasonable housing expenses paid because he didn't have or want a job. In most situations, the trustee is required to provide a reasonable housing allowance for such beneficiary even though he might be a lazy bum! Even using the word "discretion" when defining health, education, support and maintenance may not be sufficient to allow the trustee to simply say no when he or she believes the beneficiary is a bum. In other words, if you think your beneficiary might be a bum, don't use this type of a provision. The "bum provision" falls under the third item listed above, which is a true discretionary provision.

A true discretionary provision is one in which the language of the trust makes it very clear that it is up to the sole and absolute discretion of the trustee to decide whether the beneficiary is entitled to receive any of the trust's income. The person setting up the trust can put guidelines in place for the trustee. But generally, for this type of provision, it is very clear that the trustee will ultimately make the decision, and it cannot be challenged.

If you appoint a bank or trust company to serve as trustee of a trust with discretionary provisions, it will likely cost more than if you create a trust that provides for an automatic income payout. In a discretionary trust, the trustee is required to exercise more due diligence and gather more information to properly assess whether to make distributions. Since those distribution requests can occur on a regular basis, the trustee's time investment can be much more significant with a discretionary trust than with a simple income trust.

In addition to income provisions, of course, also consider what to do with the principal of the trust. Using the Apple example, we started with $100,000 and ended up with $102,000 of principal after the first year. Most trusts will give access to the principal, but that is certainly not required. Some trusts may be drafted so that only income can be used to satisfy the beneficiary's needs. The goal of those trusts is to protect the trust assets from ever being eliminated or depleted. If principal can be used to satisfy beneficiary's needs, then — depending on the degree of those needs — the principal can begin to be depleted. That can be a slippery slope toward the trust being fully exhausted.

Some examples of provisions for use of the principal, if they are to be included at all, are:

1. A 5% discretionary withdrawal right by the beneficiary;

2. Distributions for health, education, support and maintenance;

3. Incentive provisions; or

4. Discretion as exercised by the trustee, other individual or committee.

The 5% clause is something I use a lot in trusts. Often, I will not have a provision for the payout of income but instead have this 5% beneficiary discretionary withdrawal right. The 5% is based on the value of the trust estate on a given date. The payout is then made first from the income. Then, if the income is not sufficient to reach the 5% calculation, the principal is used.

The advantage of the 5% discretionary right gives the beneficiary a significant degree of control over the distributions he or she may receive. If I have four children, I may have one child who has no immediate income needs and defers distributions for a "rainy day." This allows more of the beneficiary's assets to be protected by the trust against spousal rights, creditors and eventual inheritance and estate taxation, if applicable.

With a 5% withdrawal right, you may think that the trust will eventually be exhausted. You have to consider, however, that the trust should be earning income and, hopefully, have principal appreciation. Is it reasonable to think the trust will earn interest income, dividend income and growth in stocks or other invested assets that amount to a 5% total return? If the trust is invested professionally in some type of a balanced portfolio over a long period of time, it certainly is reasonable to anticipate that, on average, the trust will grow in excess of 5% per year. If that occurs, the 5% payout will not deplete the trust. In fact, if the trust has total return (interest and dividend income and principal appreciation) in excess of 5%, as the trust grows, the 5% withdrawal right — if exercised each year — will actually be a larger amount than the previous years.

For example, if the trust earns 7% in a given year, and at the end of that year only 5% was paid out, then the second year the trust will begin with a larger principal amount than the start of the previous year. This means that if you have a similar 7% return the second year, the trust will continue to grow slightly. This will be a bit of an "inflation" protection.

The other provisions listed above for principal distributions are similar to those discussed for income provisions. The only difference is that they relate to distributions of principal instead of income.

The advantage of income and/or principal provisions that are solely discretionary upon the trustee is that the trustee can take into account factors and circumstances that occur many years after the trust is established.

The problem with discretionary trusts is finding someone who will be able to make reasonable decisions relative to distributions to your loved ones. Many families struggle with finding the perfect individual(s) or entity.

In my practice, I generally allow an adult beneficiary to have a 5% discretionary withdrawal right, with access to the balance of the trust for health, education, support and maintenance needs. The way I address issues related to generations beyond the initial beneficiary is to build in flexibility that allows the children to appoint the assets out of their trust into new trusts for the benefit of their children. This can be done with powers they can exercise during their lifetime (called "inter vivos," special powers of appointment) or via provisions in their will to take effect at their death (called a "testamentary" special power of appointment). Putting these powers in a child's trust will give that child the ability to take future circumstances into account when ultimately deciding how those assets will pass to subsequent generations.

End of Lawyers? No. When it comes to working with numerous technical and, many times, complicated trust provisions, combined with the importance of your family who is to benefit under those trusts, there really is no replacement for a qualified and experienced attorney.

CHAPTER 12

Family Dynamics: Savers (Parents) vs. Spenders (Children)

If you have a bad lawyer,
why not get a new one?

*Changing lawyers is like moving
to a different deck chair
on the Titanic.*

It has been my experience that there are generally two groups of people in this world — spenders and savers. If you don't know which one you are, just ask your parents or your in-laws. They know.

If you're a child and ever expect to receive a gift during the lifetime of your parents, you better hope that you are perceived as being a saver. If you're perceived as being a spender, or if any of your siblings are perceived as spenders, you may be out of luck when it comes to receiving any major gifts during Mom and Dad's lifetime.

In many families, making gifts to children does not come naturally. There are a couple of reasons for that. First off, parents may be concerned that if they give too much away, they won't have enough to live on. The last thing a parent wants to do is to go begging to their children for financial help. The second reason is that parents don't want to see money wasted right before their eyes. It's one thing if I leave you something in my will and you waste it. I'm not around to know about it. But if I make a gift to you during my lifetime and you blow my hard-earned money, it's not going to make me very happy.

Let me give you a couple of examples of things you may be doing that might make your parents perceive you as a spender.

1. You get a new car every two years. You may work out a good deal with your buddy at the auto dealership and set up a two-year lease. But contrast that to your parents, who may get a new vehicle every eight to 10 years, and even then they buy a car that has a few miles on it.

2. You decide to sell your 1,900-square-foot home and upgrade after just a few years because you, your spouse and three kids have outgrown it. In contrast, unless your parents have moved around a lot or have transitioned into a patio home, independent living

apartment, assisted living facility or nursing home, they may still be living in the house you were raised in. That may be only their first or second home since they got married. They raised three kids in a 1,600-square-foot house and were happy to do it.

When I was growing up, I received gifts on my birthday and Christmas, and that was about it. I got an Easter basket full of candy but no presents. Parents today (and I may not be excluded from this group) can find all kinds of special occasions to buy their kids gifts. Sometimes, they don't need an occasion at all.

If your parents are not generous givers but you are, that can cause problems. People who are not generous givers oftentimes do not understand those who are. This can create family conflict and impact the amount of gifts given, or whether they come at all.

To address some of the above issues and perceptions, encourage your parents to seek legal counsel to establish trusts for you and/or your siblings. The advantage of a trust is that parents can structure it to match their attitudes about spending and investing. A wise child might say to his or her parent, "I believe I should be able to spend my hard-earned money in any manner I choose. But the money that you give me should be separate, and I have no problem with you putting any gifts or inheritance I might receive in a trust with specific guidelines on how the money is spent, invested or otherwise handled."

So what do you do when you receive a gift from a parent or an in-law? Don't spend it! Ask your parents or the in-laws for their thoughts on a good investment for the money. Let the parents or in-laws be involved in how you invest their gift.

It may seem counter-productive to take money that your parents or in-laws want you to spend and then not spend it. Your parents or in-laws may even say that they think it's fine for you to spend it. Still, don't spend it. My advice is to pay down debt or make an investment, but don't spend it.

So what if you are the parent who is trying to decide whether to make a gift to your children? In general, I would encourage you to make gifts if you can afford to do so. Make them in small blocks, however. Make the gifts in such a fashion that if your kids do blow the money, there is still plenty of time to stop the gifting and thus stop the spending.

If my clients plan to make a fairly substantial gift, I may have them make the gift into a trust for the benefit of the child, then immediately invest some or all of the assets that were "gifted" into the trust in a single-member LLC owned by the trust. If you set up the trust so that you can be your own trustee (many of our irrevocable trusts are set up that way) you ultimately control the LLC that is 100% owned by the trust.

The trustee can appoint the manager of the LLC, so make your son or daughter the manager of the LLC held by his or her trust. Transfer the amount of assets that you are willing to let your son or daughter handle into the trust. If the child makes bad decisions, you as trustee can always remove the child as manager. If the child manages the money well, and additional assets remain in the trust, those assets can then be pushed (funded) into the LLC.

This approach is a good way to gauge how your children will handle the responsibility of managing additional assets. It's also a good opportunity for you guide them in what, for many children, will be a learning process.

When it comes to making gifts, however, income tax issues (primarily those related to basis "step-up" discussed in Chapter 20) should be considered. With the higher estate tax exemption,[5]

---

5 In 2015, the federal estate tax lifetime exemption per individual is $5,430,000. So a married couple will be entitled to a total of $10,860,000 of estate tax exemptions that can be used during their lives or upon their deaths. Each time a gift to anyone (other than to a spouse) exceeds the annual exclusion ($14,000/year in 2015), the portion of the gift over the annual exclusion will reduce the available lifetime exemption of the giver.

the need to make gifts for estate tax savings purposes is no longer a factor, except for the few with very large estates. Consequently, the income tax impact of gifting must be taken into account.

__End of Lawyers?__ Not necessarily. While you may be able to use your own judgment about making gifts to your children, an attorney can help address the tax issues and will be better equipped to set up a trust that meets all of your needs.

CHAPTER 13

Hurry Up and Wait: Planning that Prevents Your Descendants from Just Sitting Around, Waiting on Their Inheritance

How does an attorney sleep?

Jamie Hargrove

*First he lies on one side
and then lies on the other.*

I often tell my clients that they should use their estate to help their children and grandchildren become successful, not simply rich. How do you do that? That's what this chapter is about.

Your first challenge is to consider a variety of circumstances. Try to brainstorm all of the potential good, bad and ugly situations that could happen to your kids, grandkids and future generations. Does your estate plan, and particularly the trusts you establish, anticipate all of the "what ifs?" If you are just starting the estate planning process, has your attorney pointed out some of the potential problems that might develop?

Here are a few of the challenges that your descendants may face:

- Divorce
- Death with estate passing to a spouse who then remarries
- Dependency issues (drugs, alcohol, gambling)
- The descendant/beneficiary remains unemployed by choice, living off monthly trust payments
- The descendant/beneficiary's spouse exercises all the controls that were intended for the beneficiary and drains the trust on frivolous spending
- The descendant/family member withdraws as much as possible from the trust for frivolous living
- The descendant/beneficiary uses the funds to spoil the next generation, creating another generation moving toward frivolous spending and non-productive lifestyles
- A descendant/beneficiary is not yet incompetent but is on rapid decline, and in the meantime makes bad decisions with his or her access to trust assets

The above are just a few examples of the challenges facing families in estate planning. Of course, the question becomes, "How do we design a plan that will deal with all of these and other potentially destructive issues?"

The key to addressing these issues is flexibility, and using a blend of clearly articulated goals and provisions with a trustee and an advisory committee structure that can modify and redefine the rights of a trust beneficiary. The best way to address these issues is through a trust arrangement. Assets held outright have little hope of being utilized for the benefit of a family member and will more likely be used to his or her detriment.

A trust can be structured to have various categories of rights and benefits for a beneficiary (a friend, son or daughter, grandchild, etc.). For example, there may be a provision for rights and benefits that gives a lot of control and access directly to a beneficiary. The trust could then include a secondary block of rights that is more restrictive. A third block may be solely a discretionary benefit, which means the trustee, distribution or advisory committee will make decisions based on what they believe is right for a particular beneficiary. While one might argue that the trust could simply start out as a "discretionary trust," I prefer to have tiers of designated rights and access so that if a beneficiary is acting responsibly with the funds in the trust, they can maintain control. Only when the beneficiary acts irresponsibly does the second tier of discretionary clauses take effect.

As I discussed in Chapter 11, the challenge with a discretionary trust is that the decision-maker may not be clear on exactly what the person setting up the trust wanted to do. It also leaves the beneficiary wondering from year to year how much he or she will receive from the trust.

Again, if there are issues or problems with the beneficiary based on some of the concerns expressed above, the discretionary trust is the right way to go. If the trust is a multi-generational one, however, the problems you have with the current generation may not exist for the following generation. In that case, the trust can be designed to revert back to a trust where the rights of a beneficiary are specifically and clearly outlined, allowing the beneficiary to better plan for his or her financial future.

Another way of building flexibility into a trust uses what is called an "inter vivos (or lifetime) special power of appointment." A special power of appointment, as discussed in Chapters 11 and 15, is simply a way for a person (possibly even a beneficiary) to appoint assets during his or her lifetime to anyone the trust designates. A similar power is called a "testamentary special power of appointment." It is like the lifetime power except that it is exercised using a provision in the power holder's Last Will and Testament.

As an example, my parents left my inheritance to me in trust. The trust provided that if I did not leave a will with any special provision relating to this trust, the assets would pass on to my children, also in trust. However, the terms of that trust granted me a testamentary special power to appoint the assets at my death (pursuant to my will) to, or for the benefit of, my children. This gives me the ability to change the trust plan originally set up by my parents.

When my parents set up their trust plan, my children were very young, so we had no idea what their situations might be as they got older, got married, had kids, etc. Now that three of my four children are grown and on their own, I can create a trust plan that better fits their situations and appoint the assets out of the trust my parents set up for me into new trusts for my children. All of this will take effect at my death.

I am a fan of multi-generational trusts. Those trusts can offer great flexibility for future contingencies and can be a very effective way to safely transfer wealth, while providing most of the protections you need.

End of Lawyers? Not in this area. The key to maximizing the type of flexibility a trust can provide is having an attorney who understands the different types of powers and is willing to take the time to work with you to put them in place.

CHAPTER 14

Children's Inheritance: How Much Is Too Much?

Santa Claus, the tooth fairy, an honest lawyer, and an old drunk were walking along when they simultaneously spotted a hundred-dollar bill laying in the street.

Who gets it?

Jamie Hargrove

The old drunk, of course.

*The other three are
mythological creatures.*

I have talked about trusts and, in particular, leaving an inheritance for your children in a manner where it will be protected from the claims and rights of spouses or creditors and from eventual taxation in their estates. I have also talked about incentive trusts that are designed to incentivize children to be more responsible.

What I have not discussed, however, is whether you truly want to transfer your entire wealth to your children. Most of my clients tend to assume that's what they should do. Many times, however, simply asking the question, "How much is too much?" as it relates to your children's inheritance opens up a thought process that many of my clients have not previously considered.

Based on the economic situation of a particular client, I will ask what he or she thinks about their children having an additional cash flow equal to a certain amount. So, for example, I might ask, "What are your thoughts about each of your children having $50,000 a year in additional cash flow?" Often, my clients say, "That's probably fine, but I certainly wouldn't want it to be any more than that." If their children's inheritance will produce through investments, say, four or five times that amount, then my clients need to carefully consider how much is too much.

You need to ask yourself, "What will my children use this added cash flow for?" Is it going to enrich their lives? Is it going to encourage them to contribute more to their communities, to society? Will it bring them enrichment and happiness?

Everyone's situation is different. It's important, particularly when children or grandchildren are involved, to really put a pencil to what the future might look like when you (or you and your spouse) are gone and the nice estate you accumulated is passed down and consumed. If you have saved and sacrificed your entire life, yet you do not see a similar discipline in your children, the question of "how much is too much" is potentially even more important.

Jamie Hargrove

Of course, the first step is to prepare a quick calculation of exactly how much, counting your life insurance, the proceeds from the sale of your home, etc., your children will actually inherit and have to invest. If your estate is going to be subject to estate taxes, those need to be estimated and subtracted. Keep in mind that, with estate tax exemptions so much higher now, there is a pretty good chance your children will have much more cash flow to live on than you ever did. By the time they receive their inheritance, your children will likely already have homes, so they will sell your home. Your home has never produced cash flow for you, but it will produce cash flow for your children. Your life insurance has been simply an expense and has produced zero cash flow for you. It will produce new cash flow for your children. So again, you need to look at what it is that you're passing to your children and how it should best be handled by them.

Had my parents been wealthy, I would have loved for them to have passed a significant portion of my inheritance to me via a family foundation or a donor-advised fund through a community foundation or other national foundation, allowing me the right to direct which charities would benefit. This is a great way to encourage a legacy of giving.

This discipline of taking an inventory of your assets and, particularly, the future value of those assets available for investment to support your children, is a very important step. It has always amazed me that many of my clients significantly underestimate the size of their estates. They have not taken such an inventory or considered the added cash flow their estates will generate when they are gone, once their homes are liquidated and life insurance has been paid.

If you're working with a financial planner, it would be great to have him or her plug your numbers into some spreadsheets or other software that will provide forecasting and more detailed analysis. If you already have a financial advisor, I encourage you to request this service. If you don't have a financial advisor and can afford one, I encourage you to seek one out.

If you do not have a financial advisor and you feel that you cannot afford one, simply compile a complete listing of your assets and, in particular, the estimated value of those assets at the time of your death. This process is not an exact science. Your estate, and its value, will change constantly. Even the most precise forecast done through software modeling is not going to perfectly forecast your situation. There are too many assumptions that have to be made.

However, once you have tallied all of your assets and estimated the total inheritance your children will receive, play with that number a bit based on how much you think those numbers might grow during your remaining lifetime. If you're living on your assets, and they have zero growth, the number you have arrived at is probably accurate. If, on the other hand, you feel the value of your home, investments and other assets in your estate may grow, use the "Rule of 72s" to quickly calculate what the value of your estate might be 10, 20 or 30 years in the future.

The Rule of 72s is a simple process to calculate how often your estate will double in value. Here is the formula:

$$\frac{72}{\textbf{Estimated Rate of Growth}} = \begin{array}{c} \textbf{Number of Years for} \\ \textbf{Assets to Double in Value} \end{array}$$

As an example, you might tell me that you think your assets will grow 3% to 4% per year. When we talk about "growth," we are really talking about the income your estate generates, plus principal appreciation, less expenditures and income taxes. If your estate is mostly liquid in bonds and CDs, most of your income will be subject to taxes, which need to be taken into account when determining the net growth value, after taxes, of your estate. If, on the other hand, you have mostly non-income-producing real estate but that real estate is likely to continue to appreciate, such appreciation will occur without any taxes. In that situation, you're not going to have to worry about subtracting income taxes when determining a reasonable annual growth rate for your estate.

If you were to tell me that your estate is going to grow between 3% and 4%, I would suggest we use 3.6%. The nice thing about 3.6% is that it divides perfectly into 72, 20 times. What this means is that every 20 years, your estate will double in value. So if you are age 45, you're married and you think one of the two of you will reach age 85, and if you are comfortable that your estate will grow 3.6%, on average, year in and year out, your estate should double twice between now and your deaths in 40 years.

If you were to tell me that you believe your estate should grow at somewhere around 7% or 8%, I would suggest you project it based on 7.2%, which means that when you divide 72 by 7.2% you get 10. This means that, every 10 years, your estate will double.

If you are fortunate enough to have an estate that may grow as much as 10% per year, it is going to double every 7.2 years, which means that in 21 ½ years, your estate will have doubled three times. That means that in 21 ½ years, a $2 million estate will become a $16 million estate. You might think that's impossible, but it's not. You can chart it on a spreadsheet or use fancy, sophisticated software, and it will calculate that, in less than 22 years, your $2 million will grow to $16 million. Here is how it works:

- $2 million becomes $4 million in 7.2 years;
- $4 million becomes $8 million in another 7.2 years; and
- $8 million becomes $16 million in another 7.2 years,
- thus, $2 million becomes $16 million in 21 ½ years.

The rule of 72s is an easy, yet very effective tool to use in planning for your estate and retirement. It can also project what the future inheritance will look like for your children. When you start compounding your estate in this fashion, the "How much is too much?" question can suddenly take on an even more important significance.

End of Lawyers? Yes. Unfortunately lawyers do not tend to get into this analysis nearly as often or as well as financial planners. While some lawyers do, and certainly more lawyers could, the fact is that everything discussed in this chapter can be done by a non-lawyer. As time goes on, with both online tools and financial planners becoming more sophisticated, the need for the lawyers in this area will decrease substantially.

ADVANCED TRUST PLANNING

CHAPTER 15

Dynasty Trusts

---

*What do you call it when 20 lawyers
are taken to sea and thrown overboard?*

Jamie Hargrove

A good start.

For purposes of this book, a "dynasty trust" refers to a trust with a perpetual existence under relevant state law. Alaska and Delaware were among the first states to create legislation that allowed for perpetual trusts. However, in states that have not adopted specific legislation dealing with the creation of perpetual trusts, attorneys often refer to any trust that exists for more than one generation as a dynasty trust.

When creating a trust that potentially is going to last forever, there are several issues that, while important in most trust planning, should be addressed in even greater detail. The first issue is the importance of building in flexibility for future generations. This is because provisions that work for an existing, "known" generation may not work for certain individuals in future generations. As I discussed in Chapters 11 and 13, one of the important provisions we like to include in any family protection trust is a limited testamentary power of appointment for most beneficiaries. This would allow, for example, each of your children to redirect how the assets for their children eventually are held in trust. So, if the default beneficial provisions are broad, each generation can tighten the provisions for future beneficiaries. This might be done for a future beneficiary who has had a history of substance abuse, mental illness, poor fiscal management, etc. Generally, someone fitting such a profile is going to need a trust that is much more restrictive.

However, establishing powers of appointment is not necessarily a complete fix in this scenario. For example, if a grandchild has substance abuse issues, you might not want to leave control in the grandchild's hands as to how the assets pass to his or her descendants. It is in this situation that simply providing power or control to a beneficiary in one generation to direct how assets pass to the next generation may not be prudent.

An alternative (or sometimes additional) method of long-term oversight is to provide certain discretionary powers to an individual or committee who are not beneficiaries of the relevant trust. Some examples are as follows:

- **<u>Discretionary powers granted to trustee</u>**: The simplest solution is to create discretionary trusts in which the trustee has the discretion to make or withhold distributions based on circumstances outlined by you in the trust. The trust can go into great detail about any concerns, issues or scenarios that you want to address, but generally you are leaving the trustee with complete discretion to make distributions of income and/or principal.

- **<u>Use of a trust protector</u>**: While a "trust protector" is often used for administrative changes to a trust, it can also be used to direct or redirect assets within the trust. One possibility, for example, is to have two different trusts under two separate articles within your agreement. One provides broad discretionary powers to a trustee for situations that require a lot of discretion, due to substance abuse or other issues. The other provides the beneficiary with more control and access to income and principal. The trust protector can simply transfer assets between the two trusts based on the circumstances.

- **<u>Advisory committee</u>**: An "advisory committee" can provide advice or direction to a trustee. The committee can provide binding directions that require the trustee to take its advice, or its directives can be non-binding, which means that the committee gives recommendations, but the trustee makes the final decision. In this situation, there may be a corporate trustee, like a bank or trust company, while select family members or friends may make up the advisory committee. The friends or family members will be more attuned to problems or issues with the beneficiaries (kids, grandkids, etc.) than the trustee. The committee can then advise or direct the trustee based on their personal knowledge.

- **Distribution committee**: A "distribution committee" is also often made up of close friends or family members. Like an advisory committee, the distribution committee is not responsible for day-to-day investment of the trust assets or oversight of the trust. Its sole focus is directing distributions to one or more of the beneficiaries. If the trust is a discretionary trust, such discretion can be held by the distribution committee rather than by the trustee.

Since a dynasty trust can last forever, it is important to create mechanisms that will allow your chosen management and oversight structures to continue over the long term. One of the ways my firm does that is by creating self-perpetuating committees. The advisory and distribution committees discussed above are often three-person committees. We provide that the committee is self-perpetuating, meaning that if a person is unable or unwilling to serve as a committee member, the two remaining members will select, by unanimous agreement, the replacement member.

Once you communicate your goals, concerns and desires for your planning, a skilled estate planning attorney should be able to mix and match the above scenarios to create a good fit for your family.

Another important consideration for a dynasty trust is to provide a mechanism to remove and replace the trustee. An individual named as a trustee or successor trustee may be perfectly fine today but, at some future point, he or she may have diminished capacity, personal financial problems or other issues that could taint his or her desirability to handle money and serve in such an important position. Reasons may also develop that make a once-trusted corporate trustee (bank or trust company) undesirable (change of ownership, merger, employee turnover, etc.). For example, your family may have a relationship with a specific individual at a particular institution. That individual may relocate to a different institution, retire, etc., so you find yourself working with individuals who give less than desirable service, offer diminished performance or have very different fee arrangements. In any of these situations, you want to have a way to remove and replace the trustee. I recommend that an advisory committee be designated to hold this power.

Some trusts will allow beneficiaries the right to change trustees. This is better than not having any way to remove and replace a trustee. My personal preference, however, is to give a committee such power, with at least one person on the committee being independent of the family. It may be your attorney, CPA, financial advisor or a close family friend. This committee has no daily responsibilities. Its job is only to act when there is a problem.

Another issue to consider with a dynasty trust is the impact of the multiplicity of trusts as generations pass. If you have two children, and each child in each succeeding generation has two children, then in just six more generations the total number of trusts will approach 200.

When you incorporate powers of appointment allowing your children to determine how assets pass to the generations after them, consider including the ability to give to charitable organizations. If you have someone in a future generation who has no children and becomes very active in a worthy cause, you may want to give him or her the ability to pass some or all of his or her trust to that cause or charity. You may also have descendants who do not want to pass large trusts on to their children for any number of reasons and would prefer to give back to their community.

The dynasty trust is a great tool. It adds complexity, in that you need to consider a lot more "what ifs" than in other types of trust planning. However, if properly set up to reflect your goals and intentions, it can be a remarkable way to leave a lasting legacy.

End of Lawyers? No. If you're going to create a dynasty trust, you need to have an attorney assist you. Online DIY services, unless very specialized like the NetLaw system, are not going to provide much guidance or assistance with this type of complex trust planning.

CHAPTER 16

The Domestic Asset Protection Trust

*Why do they bury lawyers 20 feet deep
instead of 6 feet?*

Because deep, deep, deep down, lawyers are pretty good people.

A Domestic Asset Protection Trust (DAPT) is an asset protection trust created in one of several states. For some, the term "Delaware Trust" has become a more general reference to the DAPT. It's a bit like when you order a "coke" — you may not necessarily mean that you want a Coke® product, just that you want a cola.

While Delaware was not the first state to adopt DAPT legislation, it was on the heels of the first. The first state to innovate a state statutory structure allowing DAPTs was Alaska in 1995. Not long after Alaska approved DAPTs, I began drafting and working with Alaska attorneys to perfect a planning tool and provide the benefits of such planning to my clients in Kentucky. A year or so later, Delaware came roaring out with DAPT legislation.

Prior to Alaska starting the trend for domestic (U.S.) asset protection trusts, it was necessary to use an "offshore," or foreign, asset protection trust. The foreign trust continues to be a viable option that may be more effective at protecting assets, but it is also more expensive.

Because of abuses in the use of foreign trusts — attempts to shift federal income tax to a trust to eliminate U.S. taxation on it (this never works!) — the federal government created certain reporting requirements that relate to foreign trusts. While there are some work-arounds with foreign trusts, more and more asset protection attorneys are finding that DAPT legislation attempts to provide the same protections and planning opportunities as foreign trusts but with much less disclosure and reporting to the federal government and the IRS. I say "attempts" because there are certain constitutional arguments concerning the degree of protection DAPTs offer that have yet to be fully vetted and battle-tested through the federal court system.

Delaware had the benefit of taking what Alaska had done and improving upon it. What Delaware has that Alaska does not is its chancery court, which for almost 20 years has distinguished Delaware from the other 14 states that now have asset protection statutes. As of this printing, there are 15 states with asset protection statutes. They are:

1. Alaska
2. Delaware
3. Hawaii
4. Mississippi
5. Missouri
6. Nevada
7. New Hampshire
8. North Dakota
9. Ohio
10. Oklahoma
11. Rhode Island
12. South Dakota
13. Tennessee
14. Utah
15. Virginia

So why does the chancery court distinguish Delaware from the pack? The chancery court in Delaware is a separate court system set aside exclusively for trust and corporate matters. The judges in that court system are appointed based on a background in either trust or corporate practice, or both.

What this means is that if you have established a Delaware asset protection trust, and you now have creditors attacking the trust, the chances of you getting a judge who actually understands the statutory nature of the DAPT is virtually a given in Delaware. In nearly every other state, good luck! Of course, if you never have to go to court and use the laws of a particular state to protect your assets, then you'll never realize this significant difference. But if you're putting your assets in a trust with the primary purpose of creditor protection, it's hard to argue that there is any domestic jurisdiction that rivals the superior asset protection that Delaware provides. While the statutes of a particular state are important — and states will often brag that their statutes are better than another state's — when it comes to the implementation and enforcement of those provisions, no state other than Delaware can really tout it has the superior platform.

If, on the other hand, you already have a potential claim headed your way, Delaware may not be your best bet. If some event has already triggered a potential claim against you, planning is still available, but only within clearly defined guidelines. But note that in these situations, Tennessee is actually the best jurisdiction to use, simply because it has a 6-month statute of limitations related to the transfers. Tennessee, like several other states, has a standard two-year statute. But with "notice," you can shorten that to six months. Some legal experts in this area suggest that a local public record filing is sufficient notice to trigger the shorter six-month statute. Regardless, Delaware has a four-year statute. And if you are about to be chased, you want to have the shortest road ahead before you can exit the race! Tennessee gives you that quicker exit.

The introduction of DAPTs also brought state income tax planning opportunities. You can transfer certain assets to the DAPT in order to shift the tax situs (i.e., location) to the state hosting the DAPT. The advantage lies in when a DAPT state has no state income tax. Some states, like Florida and Tennessee, have no state income tax on individuals or trusts. Other states, like Delaware, do not have a state income tax for non-residents or beneficiaries of trusts who are non-residents.

Before the advent of DAPTs, the ability to transfer the tax situs from an individual's home state where there are income taxes into a trust in a state where there are no income taxes was impossible to do. State revenue cabinets said that if a creditor could get to your assets, even if the assets were in a trust in another state, the state taxing authority could also get to those assets. When the DAPT came along and prevented creditors from gaining access to its assets, suddenly there was an argument — and a very good argument — that states could not tax activities in those types of trusts. The DAPT therefore can be a tool for individuals who are planning to sell a business or a low-basis marketable security. It allows them to sell the business or security without triggering state income tax. This can amount to significant income tax savings for large transactions.

When it comes to using a DAPT for state income tax planning, the tables are a bit turned. Some of the other asset protection states are as good as, if not better than, Delaware. Delaware statutes have created a requirement for a work-around related to some recent rulings. States with more recent asset protection legislation have addressed the problems Delaware had in its statute. Regardless, the court system that makes Delaware a hands-down choice for asset protection is not as relevant when you're talking about simply providing state income tax planning. I find, for example, that Tennessee has become a good jurisdiction for the state income tax planning involved in DAPTs.

The way that a DAPT is used to avoid state income tax is to transfer the asset to the DAPT prior to its sale and prior to any agreements that are **binding** for the sale of such asset. So, if I'm going to sell my family business in a stock sale, I want to transfer my stock to my DAPT before I enter into any binding sales agreement. The good news is that many early agreements (sometimes called letters of intent) are not binding for purposes of this issue. They may bind the seller to certain confidentiality terms and prohibit the seller from selling to anyone else during a defined time period, but they do not obligate the buyer to buy or the seller to sell. In those situations, the stock in the company could be transferred to the DAPT.

Once the family-owned stock (or partnership or LLC units) or low-basis marketable securities are in the trust, they can be sold. If the trust jumps through some other hoops relative to its design and the tax treatment of the trust, the sale will be taxed to the trust, pursuant to the state laws governing the trust. If the state laws impose no income tax on the transaction, it will close without triggering any state income taxes.

There are a lot of details and issues with state income tax planning that are beyond the scope of this chapter. The goal of this chapter is simply to raise the issue and give you some understanding of how and why this planning works. You then need to seek out a tax and trust attorney with specific competence in this type of planning.

End of Lawyers? No. If there was ever an area where you need a lawyer to assist in a particular type of planning, this is it. While corporate trust departments in DAPT states provide great expertise and some degree of planning oversight, they are not going to be a replacement for a knowledgeable tax and asset protection lawyer.

CHAPTER 17

Grantor Trusts: My Favorite Trusts

What did the lawyer name his daughter?

Sue.

This chapter is for individuals (or their advisors) interested in advanced planning for larger estates. Generally, you will need to have an estate of several million dollars before the discussion in this chapter will be relevant. If that's not you, you may want to skip this chapter and the next couple as well.

A grantor trust is a trust that, for income tax purposes, is treated as owned by an individual. In most cases, such individual, or "grantor," is the person who sets up (or funds) the trust. A reference to a "grantor trust" generally is a reference to a trust that the IRS treats as non-existent for income tax purposes. In other words, the IRS takes the position that a grantor trust does not have its own separate tax status. This means that any income earned by the trust's assets is reportable by the grantor and not the trust itself or its beneficiaries. The trust is essentially ignored. As mentioned above, the "grantor" is usually the person who establishes the trust. However, in some situations, a beneficiary may be treated as the "grantor."

Most professionals are comfortable with treating a revocable trust (i.e., a revocable living trust) as a grantor trust. The confusion arises, however, when irrevocable trusts are treated as grantor trusts. It seems unnatural that an irrevocable trust, designed to be outside the grantor's estate for gift and estate tax purposes, could effectively be ignored for income tax purposes under these grantor trust rules.

When the grantor trust rules were adopted (in the early 1950s), trusts had previously been used to shift taxable income either to the trust itself, where the income tax rates were once much lower than individual rates, or to individual beneficiaries of such trusts who might be in lower income tax brackets. As a result, it became common practice to use trusts to shift income to a lower tax bracket. The 1950s federal legislation ushered in a dramatic change to that income tax planning technique. These laws have changed little since their enactment.

Even though these rules have been around a long time,

many tax professionals are only now beginning to fully understand all of their intricacies, mainly as a result of a tremendous increase in the number of irrevocable trusts being created. The rules are complex, but when used correctly, they can accomplish a lot of creative planning.

It should be noted that the designation of a trust as a grantor trust is only applicable to income taxes and has no impact on whether the assets in a trust are includable in the grantor's estate for gift and estate tax purposes. This fact, however, is still hard for many professionals, and sometimes even some IRS agents, to get their arms around. But it is this fact that makes grantor trusts such a unique planning tool. See Chapter 22 for a more detailed discussion of the income tax consequences of grantor trusts.

End of Lawyers? No. This is very complex planning that requires an attorney with very specialized expertise. Many estate planning attorneys may do little to no planning in this area, so search for the right attorney to make sure you are being exposed to all the options available for your situation.

CHAPTER 18

Grantor Trusts: Advanced Planning Techniques

What's the difference between a lawyer and a herd of buffalo?

The lawyer charges more.

This chapter will focus on using grantor trusts as a central part of advanced estate planning techniques. Because a grantor trust is ignored for income tax purposes, there are some significant opportunities available.

The most popular way to use grantor trusts in advanced planning is to trigger the grantor's sale of his or her discounted assets to his or her grantor trust. Since the grantor is treated as the "owner" of such trust, the sale is ignored for income tax purposes. See Chapter 22 regarding tax treatment of grantor trusts. The goal is often to move assets that have a great likelihood for appreciation out of the grantor's estate for gift and estate tax purposes, without having to use any of the grantor's federal gift tax exemption. The reason no exemption is needed is because it is utilized only when there is a gift. If the transaction is a "sale" and not a "gift," we are simply swapping one asset (e.g., non-voting company stock) for another asset (e.g., cash or a note receivable due from the trust). Thus, at least as to the sale portion of the transaction, there is no gift and therefore no use of exemption.

Examples of "discounted" assets often used for this planning are:

- Non-voting interests in closely held companies
- Non-voting interests in a real estate family limited liability company (FLLC) or limited partnership interests in a real estate family limited partnership (FLP)
- Non-voting interests in a securities-only FLLC or FLP
- Undivided interest in real estate (e.g., a 50% joint ownership in a piece of rental property)

When valued for tax purposes, "discounts" will apply, thereby reducing the value of the asset being "gifted" or sold to the grantor trust. For example, a non-voting ownership interest in an entity is less valuable than a voting interest. Discounts for "lack of marketability," "closely held business" and other discounts can all add up to a significant reduction in the value of the business or real estate interests being moved out of your taxable estate.

Once the asset being transferred is valued, it can either be "gifted" or sold to the grantor trust. As mentioned above, structuring the trust as a grantor trust will allow the sale to occur without triggering an income-taxable event. While the sale is recognized as a completed transfer out of the grantor's estate for gift and estate tax purposes, the sale is ignored for income tax purposes. This allows a "freeze" of any or all assets that are sold to the grantor trust at what may be a very conservative (discounted) valuation. All future appreciation on such assets being transferred (whether by gift or by sale) will occur outside of the grantor's taxable estate. In a leveraged sale (discussed further below), the assets sold will be replaced with a promissory note equal to the conservative valuation and at a fixed interest rate.

A leveraged sale to a grantor trust involves the trust giving a promissory note as part of the payment for the purchase. The note is generally secured with the assets of the trust, including a security interest in the asset just purchased. The interest on the note is non-taxable to the grantor and is non-deductible by the trust when accrued or paid. Since the sales transaction is between the grantor and his or her grantor trust, not only is the initial sales transaction ignored, the repayment of the note is also ignored for income tax purposes. Of course, for estate and gift tax purposes, the terms of the note should be strictly adhered to since the note will remain an asset in the taxable estate for estate tax purposes. This planning is illustrated as follows:

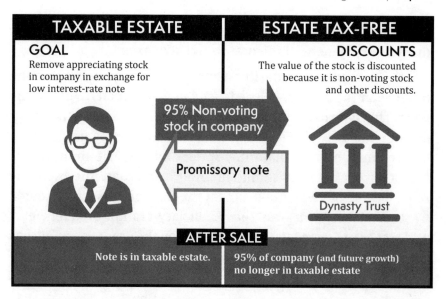

The sales transaction should be structured, if possible, to avoid any argument that it is too thinly capitalized. It is best to capitalize the grantor trust initially with a gift of assets to give the grantor trust sufficient assets to make the transaction consistent with a reasonable third-party, commercial transaction. There should be a minimum of 10% capital/equity in the grantor trust before the sales transaction is consummated. If direct equity cannot be secured, the grantor should look to someone to provide a guarantee of the note as additional security.

Since the grantor trust is ignored for income tax purposes, the grantor will be paying the taxes for the income generated by the trust. This is effectively an additional "gift" to the grantor trust equal to the value of the taxes paid by the grantor. Such gift, however, is not required to be reported as a taxable gift. This creates a pension-fund type growth opportunity for the trust. That is, the grantor trust's assets will be set to appreciate without any income tax obligation and, like a pension fund, will therefore grow at a much quicker rate. The grantor trust is not avoiding income tax since the grantor pays the tax, but it does allow for significant appreciation opportunities, while simultaneously providing the grantor a continuing reduction in his or her estate due to the payment of the grantor trust's taxes.

As mentioned earlier, there is one way that someone other than the grantor of the trust can be deemed owner of the trust. This type of grantor trust is sometimes called a beneficiary grantor trust (BGT). Treating a beneficiary as the grantor can create some unique planning opportunities. The main one is that a parent or other family member can create the BGT. The reason this is an advantage is that the BGT, because it is created by someone else, can grant the beneficiary-grantor broader rights and access to the trust's assets than when the grantor establishes the trust himself or herself.

A person can sell discounted assets to the BGT and yet retain an interest in the assets being sold. This is very complex planning, and the details are well beyond the scope of this chapter. Seek out a trained attorney who can explore this opportunity with you.

End of Lawyers? No. As you can see from this and the previous chapter, grantor trusts require the specialized expertise of a trained attorney to help you consider all the options.

CHAPTER 19

Growing an Existing Trust

What do you get when you cross a librarian with a lawyer?

All the information you need,
but you can't understand a word of it.

Many of us are not fortunate enough to be the beneficiary of a trust set up by a parent, grandparent or other family member. Those who are recipients of such good fortune should give serious consideration to whether their own investment and business opportunities should be created inside such a trust rather than in their own names.

For example, assume that I am the sole beneficiary of a trust established by my grandparents. The trust has $300,000 in it and, at my death, the assets pass on to my children.

If I am single and do not anticipate getting married, I should consider initiating the new business I am about to launch or other great investment opportunity inside the trust rather than in my own name. The appreciation and growth from such business or investment is immediately subject to the asset protections offered by the third-party trust. Yet, for that trust, I may have broad rights and access. I may also have control of the trust if I am the trustee, or at least have the power to select a trustee.

To accomplish such a plan, I simply need to use assets in the trust for some of the initial funding for the new investment or venture. It may be that there are limited funds inside the trust for this type of a business or investment. Further, the funds necessary to make an investment or start a business may be in my individual name. In this case, the new business entity or entity that is set up to purchase a piece of real estate, for example, can be owned by the trust with only a nominal amount of funding passing from the trust into a new bank account for the business or real estate LLC. That could be as little as $100. Then, I personally may make a loan to the new LLC. If there is a need for additional capital or loans, the LLC can borrow funds, with me providing a guarantee for such financing.

With most trusts, the beneficiary is stuck with the initial terms. It may not provide a lot of flexibility in terms of how assets are ultimately passed to the beneficiary's children, other family members or charitable interests. Some trusts leave the beneficiary with broad powers of appointment to redirect how the assets pass once the beneficiary dies. If such broad rights to redirect the assets are not in the trust, the beneficiary will have to get comfortable with the terms of the trust and the impact the trust will have on successor beneficiaries.

The approach discussed in this chapter only works for individuals who are already beneficiaries of a trust and are comfortable with its existing terms and confines. The key advantages are that the new investment and all of its future value may have significant protections inside the trust. The protections include allowing the new investment to be creditor-proof (as to the beneficiary's creditors), protected from spousal claims upon divorce or death, and excluded from the beneficiary's taxable estate. The protections will also relate to the new investment's growth and its earnings that are reinvested inside the trust.

End of Lawyers? No. The complexities of establishing a business or making investments within the context of an existing trust require the help of an experienced estate planning attorney.

TAX ISSUES AND TRUST TAXATION

CHAPTER 20

Step-Up in Income Tax Basis

What's the difference between a lawyer
and a leech?

Jamie Hargrove

When you die, a leech will stop
sucking your blood.

In over 30 years of practice, I cannot tell you how many times I have gotten a call from a client, friend or prospective client saying they either have already, or are about to, transfer all assets out of their parent's name because Mom or Dad is on her or his death bed. The reflex response to a sudden realization that a loved one may soon die is, "Oh, I have to get all of the assets out of his or her estate!" Most people are not exactly sure why they should get the assets out, however. Maybe they read a book on avoiding probate, or they have heard horror stories about huge taxes and think that a last-minute transfer will help them avoid inheritance and/or estate taxes.

While not always true, in most cases it is a bad idea to transfer assets out of a person's name just before death. One of the reasons is due to a loss of "step up" in income tax basis as a result of the transfer. This may sound very technical. Yes, the "step up" income tax basis rules are slightly complex, but the practical application is fairly straightforward.

Any assets that are owned (whether in an individual's name or in an individual's living trust) will receive a "step up" in income tax basis as a result of being part of the decedent's taxable estate. When I say "taxable estate," I am not referring to an estate that has to pay tax. Most estates now will not be paying any tax. No inheritance tax. No estate tax. Consequently, even though an estate is "taxable," there really are no taxes due. As discussed in Chapter 5, there are a few states that still have an inheritance tax and, of course, in very large estates you may be subject to federal estate tax. Those situations, however, are the exception, not the rule.

So what does it mean to have a "step up" in income tax basis? Assume, for example, that you bought one share of Apple stock when it was selling for $100 per share. Let's then assume that at the moment of your death, the stock was selling for $500 per share. If you die with that share of stock in your name (or titled in your living trust), the share will receive a "step up" in its income tax basis, meaning it gets a new income tax basis equal to $500 per share. Had the one share of stock been sold the day before you died, there would have been a $400 gain on the share of stock because you purchased the stock for $100, and you sold it for $500. Also, if you gift that share of stock to your son the day before you die, the son then takes a "carryover basis," which means his income tax basis would equal yours at the time of the gift. That is, you purchased it for $100, you gave it to him with a $100 basis, and if he then sells it, he will be subject to a $400 gain. Again, if your son had received the stock under your will and sold the stock any time thereafter, he would have zero gain, assuming the stock remained valued at $500 per share.

This same example works with a family farm. Assume, for example, that your grandmother and grandfather purchased a family farm many years ago for $50,000. Assume that the farm is now worth $550,000. If the family rushes in and has Granddad (or his power of attorney) transfer the farm to the kids or grandkids just before he dies, the kids or grandkids will receive the farm with the original income tax basis of $50,000. This means when Granddad dies and the property is sold, there will be a $500,000 gain on the sale of that property. Had the family not rushed in to get all the assets out of Granddad's estate, the farm would have been subject to the "step up" in basis rules, with a new basis of $550,000 when it passes out of his estate to the kids or grandkids. Doing nothing, therefore, saves the family from paying tax on a gain of $500,000.

Again, as mentioned above, there are probably no inheritance tax or estate tax consequences to having the property remain in the estate. Yet, all of a sudden, there is a huge income tax benefit to simply doing nothing. In other words, it would have been better to do nothing than to rush in, have an attorney prepare a deed and make a transfer just before Granddad's death. I cannot tell you how many times in over 30 years of practice that I have seen this very thing happen.

There is some good news, however. In my practice, I have been successful in advising that a family farm, in particular, is transferred with a "retained interest," thereby including it in the taxable estate of Mom, Dad, Grandfather or Grandmother. This goes against the general rule that transferring property or assets out of your estate means they will not be part of your taxable estate for the step-up-in-basis rules. There are a whole set of cases, however, where people have made transfers, maybe years in advance of a death, and because of a retained interest in the transfer, the IRS argued that the transferred asset (the family farm in this case) is still taxed in the estate.

Assume that, as part of basic estate planning, the family decides to get the family farm out of Granddad's estate. This planning was done when the estate tax exemption was $600,000. The concern was that the farm might appreciate beyond $600,000 and trigger a 55% estate tax. Consequently, planning was set up to have the property transferred to other family members or in trust. The farm may also be held in a family limited partnership or a family limited liability company to facilitate the planning. The problem with such planning is that you now have a situation where that farm would not have triggered inheritance or estate taxes (because of the huge, $5 million-plus estate tax exemption and no inheritance tax in most states), and yet the family loses the step up in income tax basis because the property is not part of the estate.

Perhaps there was a retained interest in use of the farm as a part of the transfer. So assume, for example, that Granddad transfers the property to his children but continues to live in the home until his death. Also assume that there was no lease of the home back to Granddad. Granddad's choice to still live on the farm is considered a "retained" interest by the IRS, which pulls the farm back into his taxable estate. Perfect! That's exactly what you want in most cases. If there had been a lease agreement in place, with Granddad paying a lease payment monthly, quarterly or annually, this argument won't work. It's when he lived on the farm rent-free that we have an argument for step up in basis.

The good news here is that, in many cases, it could be argued that such continued use of the residence by Granddad is a retained interest. Therefore, the property would be ***included*** in the taxable estate. Being included in the taxable estate may have zero tax impact for inheritance and estate tax purposes, but it offers the ability to take advantage of the step up in income tax basis on the farm. When the kids sell the family farm after Granddad dies, there will be little or no income taxes on the sale.

Another example of a retained interest may be where Granddad continues to receive income off some crops or land rental. Such retained income or interest in the profits from the farming operation would be a "retained interest" and arguably allow for the property to be included in the estate under this retained interest exception.

These step-up-in-basis rules are even important in situations where a family farm is an asset likely to be around for multiple generations. The concern, in those cases, is not the trigger of taxes when the property is ultimately sold, since the family doesn't anticipate selling the farm anytime soon. There are still, however, benefits to taking advantage of the step-up-in-basis rules.

The main reason to take advantage of the step-up-in-basis rules in this case is to get a step up in depreciable assets related to the farm. There are lots of items related to a farm (fences, roadways, outbuildings, barns, etc.) that have long been fully depreciated down to a zero basis. Working with the step-up-in-basis rules will give those depreciable items a new income tax basis and effectively allow for a restart on the depreciation to those farm improvements.

End of Lawyers? No. While the step-up-in-basis rule is fairly simple, it can have significant tax implications to a family. This issue can impact estates of all shapes and sizes, so it's essential to have an experienced attorney help you navigate these waters.

CHAPTER 21

Income Taxation of Trusts

What's the difference between
a shame and a pity?

If a busload of lawyers goes over a cliff,
and there are no survivors,
that's known as a pity.

If there were any empty seats,
that's a shame.

The taxation of trusts can be fairly complicated and involved. Various tax issues and aspects of trust taxation can be a challenge for even an accomplished CPA. This chapter will be brief and give you some simple rules related to the taxation of trusts.

The (2015) tax rates for complex trusts are as follows:

Taxable income up to $2,500	15%
Taxable income over $2,500	25%
Taxable income over $5,900	28%
Taxable income over $9,050	33%
Taxable income over $12,300	39.6%

As you can see, it doesn't take much taxable income ($12,300) inside a trust to get to a tax rate that is equal to the highest tax rate for an individual. As an individual taxpayer, you don't get to the 39.6% tax bracket (in 2015) until you have income of $413,200 (or $464,850 if married, filing jointly).

So at this point you might say, "Yikes, why would I ever want a trust?" As you'll see below, many trusts (e.g., grantor trusts and simple trusts) do not pay tax on ordinary income. Trusts that do pay tax (e.g., complex trusts) only pay tax on ordinary income items if the income is retained and not distributed to the trust's beneficiaries.

Grantor trusts are effectively ignored for income tax purposes, which I discuss in detail in Chapter 22. Trusts that are not grantor trusts fall into two categories, simple trusts and complex trusts, and are taxed as follows:

Simple trusts: A simple trust is formed by a document that requires all income in the trust to be paid to one or more beneficiaries of the trust. This type of trust (again, all income required to be distributed) will never pay taxes on ordinary income. Instead, the trust will show on its tax return that the income is distributed (or required to be distributed) to one or more beneficiaries. Those beneficiaries then receive an IRS

Schedule K–1, which will reflect the beneficiary's share of the trust's income. The trust beneficiaries are then required to report the income from the trust on their individual tax returns.

If a simple trust has capital gains triggered inside the trust, the capital gains are reported on the trust's tax return and are taxed to the trust, not to the trust's beneficiaries. In other words, a capital gain is not shown on the beneficiaries' K-1s. In very general terms, therefore, a beneficiary of a simple trust will be reporting the simple trust's interest income, dividend income or possibly other forms of ordinary income, such as rental income. If a stock or other capital asset is sold, the resulting capital gain, if any, will be reported and paid by the simple trust.

Complex trusts: A complex trust is a trust in which the income is _not_ required to be distributed to one or more beneficiaries of the trust each year.

Each year, the complex trust will either be taxed on its income earned or show the income on the IRS Schedule K–1. The determining factor for whether the trust reports and pays the tax or the beneficiary reports and pays it (via a Schedule K–1) is determined based on whether the income is actually distributed from the complex trust to the beneficiary during the tax year.

Income that is distributed is taxed to the beneficiaries. Income that is retained is taxed to the trustee at the trust income tax rate.

If trust distributions, whether out of a simple trust or a complex trust, exceed the amount of income for a given year, such distributions are considered payouts of principal and are generally not taxable.

Here are some examples of how a complex trust is taxed.

Assumption: Assume that the trust has ordinary income during the current year of $100,000. Also assume that some marketable securities are sold, triggering a capital gain of $20,000.

EXAMPLE 1:

Assume that the trust distributed $60,000 to beneficiaries in the current year. The taxation works like this:

	COMPLEX TRUST
Taxable ordinary income:	$100,000
Distributions to beneficiaries:	$60,000
Amount of ordinary income taxed to the complex trust:	$40,000 ($100,000-$60,000)
Amount of ordinary income taxed to beneficiaries:	$60,000
Amount of capital gains taxed to the complex trust:	$20,000

EXAMPLE 2:

Assume that the trust distributed $130,000 to beneficiaries in the current year. The taxation works like this:

	COMPLEX TRUST
Taxable ordinary income:	$100,000
Distributions to beneficiaries:	$130,000
Amount of ordinary income taxed to the complex trust:	-0- ($100,000-$100,000)
Amount of ordinary income taxed to beneficiaries:	$100,000
Amount of capital gains taxed to the complex trust:	$20,000

Part of a trustee's job is to take into consideration the differences, if any, in the income tax rates between the trust and a beneficiary. With a simple trust, this is not an issue since the trustee does not have an option as to where the income will be taxed. Since the taxation of a complex trust's income depends on whether there are distributions, the trustee should take the potential differences in tax rates into account.

A trustee's ability to manage taxable income between beneficiaries who may be at a lower income tax rate versus the trust at a higher rate is sometimes fairly easy, sometimes not so much. Any distributions must be consistent with the terms of the trust, which will govern the trustee's ability to make distributions. The terms of the trust, however, may grant the trustee a great degree of flexibility and, in other cases, may give very little discretion to the trustee in determining whether to make — or not make — distributions.

End of Lawyers? That depends. CPAs have often been ahead of lawyers in understanding the ins and outs of trust taxation. Certainly, there are estate planning and elder law attorneys with expertise in trust accounting and taxation. They are not as plentiful as you would hope. A good tax accountant should be able to assist in addressing some of the unique challenges of trust taxation related tax planning. If you want to do it yourself, secure a leading tax software package that includes trust forms and get comfortable with how it handles the taxation of the trust and distributions.

CHAPTER 22

Income Taxation of Grantor Trusts

How do you get a group of lawyers
to smile for a photo?

Jamie Hargrove

Just say, "Fees!"

For income tax purposes, treating a trust as a "grantor trust" can either be a good thing or a bad thing. The income tax rates for a complex trust (i.e., a non-grantor trust) and an individual are the same. However, unlike an individual who gets a gradual ascent through the "low" tax rate brackets, a trust can find its income subject to the highest income tax rate when it reaches approximately $12,000.

Remember, a grantor trust's income and capital gains are taxed to the grantor on his or her federal form 1040 and, if applicable, his or her state income tax return. A grantor trust does not pay the tax on such income. However, a non-grantor trust is treated as a distinct taxpayer. If a non-grantor trust has taxable income, either it will pay all or part of the income tax, or the beneficiaries will pay all or part of the tax. The income will **not** be taxed to **both** the trust and the beneficiaries. It will be allocated to the trust and/or beneficiaries, depending on what, if any, distributions were made from the trust to the beneficiaries during the relevant tax year. Thus, the income of a grantor trust will be taxed at the grantor's top rate, whereas the income of a non-grantor trust will be taxed at the trust's top rate *or* the beneficiaries' top rates. Accordingly, depending on the tax rates of the grantor, the trust and/or beneficiaries, a grantor trust may produce good or bad results. Here is an illustration of how the taxation works:

	GRANTOR TRUST	NON-GRANTOR
Taxable income:	$100,000	$100,000
Distributions to beneficiaries:	$40,000	$40,000
Amount taxed to grantor/settlor:	$100,000	-0-
Amount taxed to beneficiaries:	-0-	$40,000
Amount taxed to the trust:	-0-	$60,000

End of Lawyers? No way. Again, this is very complex planning and requires an attorney with specialized expertise.

UNIQUE TRUST PLANNING CIRCUMSTANCES

CHAPTER 23

Second Marriages: His Kids, Her Kids, Our Kids

How many lawyers does it take to change a lightbulb?

Jamie Hargrove

Three.

One to climb the ladder.
One to shake it.
And one to sue the ladder company.

One of the more challenging estate planning situations is a second marriage, where each spouse has his or her own children. If the second marriage produces children, that adds a little more complexity, but it mostly is the "my kids, your kids" scenario that creates potential problems.

Estate planning for a blended family is complicated by two factors. One is the "dower/curtesy rights" a spouse gains by becoming a spouse. Second is what I call the "trust me" syndrome. Dower or curtesy rights are set forth in state laws that give certain protections to a surviving husband or wife against being "disinherited." Generally, those rights accrue immediately upon marriage. In most states, the concept of non-marital or pre-marital assets is not an issue.

Here's an example of dower rights. Bob and Jane got married in a late Friday afternoon ceremony. They hopped on a red-eye to the Bahamas, arriving early Saturday morning. Bob has three children, and Jane has two children. Bob and Jane agreed long before the wedding that, upon their respective deaths, what he brought into the marriage would go to his kids, and what Jane brought into the marriage would go to her kids.

After sleeping most of Saturday, Bob and Jane decide to take a late evening swim in the ocean. Bob goes a bit too far and never returns.

There are two possible outcomes with Bob's estate. Neither is favorable to his kids. They are:

- In some states, marriage revokes a will. If Bob lives in a state that abides by this law, the Last Will and Testament he prepared years before his marriage to Jane, in which he leaves all of his estate to his kids, will now be revoked. In many states, this means that up to half of his estate will pass to his wife, rather than all of his estate passing to his kids. The fact that all of his assets were pre-marital or non-marital is irrelevant. It's also irrelevant that he and his wife were married less than 48 hours before his death. Their "verbal understanding" is also generally not enforceable.

- Let's assume that Bob was a resident of a state that did not have the "marriage revokes a will" law on its books. It's pretty likely that Jane will have what is usually called an "elective share" right. This means that Jane can elect against the will and effectively take up to half of Bob's estate. Of course, Jane might never have made the election had Bob's spoiled kids not treated her so poorly during the funeral and grieving process. Jane, as a result, has become convinced that Bob would not want his kids to get all of his assets. So like any good wife, she does what she thinks Bob would want her to do: she elects against Bob's will and takes half of his estate. Not a bad payoff for less than 48 hours of marriage.

In situations where a second marriage has been lengthy, there may be a great deal of trust between husband and wife. In those cases, the spouses intend to leave their estate to the survivor. It is assumed that the survivor will eventually leave the estate equally among all the children or in some other division that both husband and wife agreed to before either of them died.

The problem with the informal "trust me" plan is that a lot of life can happen after the death of a spouse. So, if Bob is 65 when he dies and Jane is 60, Jane could certainly live another 30 years, or even more. A lot of things can change in that time, including another marriage (or two) for Jane, a significant change in the makeup, value or nature of assets, as well as the relationships between Jane and her stepkids. When the children's father was married to their stepmom, life among them was harmonious. But once Dad is gone, the link connecting them is broken. All too often, the relationship either sours or simply is diminished by time and less frequent contact. Even in the best of situations, people's busy lives can turn a strong relationship into a virtually nonexistent one.

When Jane goes to see her attorney 30 years after Bob's death, and 10 years since she has heard from his kids, the attorney will certainly ask why a significant portion of her estate is passing to individuals she has had virtually no contact with for a decade. At that point, Jane may also have a diminished mental capacity. All of those factors combined may lead to Bob's kids being cut out of their inheritance.

A planning solution to these very difficult family situations is to consider the use of prenuptial agreements, postnuptial agreements and/or trusts. Some of my clients over the years have been opposed to any type of a marital agreement, whether prenuptial (executed before marriage) or postnuptial (executed after a marriage). Many have said that these agreements encourage or sanction divorce. This is, in fact, not usually the case. Many of the marital agreements I establish for clients do not address divorce and instead only focus on protection of assets/inheritance in the event of the death of husband or wife. I have found that, in many situations, the best plan is a combined marital and trust agreement. The trust agreement helps keep the assets clearly identified and segregated, and can provide other protections in the case of a remarriage by the surviving spouse.

In many states, for a marital agreement to be enforceable, husband and wife should have separate attorneys. Also in many states, if the husband and wife do not <u>each</u> have separate legal counsel, the agreement is very likely to be unenforceable, and the whole process is a waste of time. Bottom line, entering into any type of marital agreement requires the counsel of specialized attorneys who understand the intricacies of family law, along with the aspects of trusts and how family law and trust planning work in tandem.

Jamie Hargrove

End of Lawyers? Absolutely not! Someday, there may be online systems that will easily address all the second marriage issues that couples encounter, but such a service is not available now. If there is ever a need for a trained lawyer, it's during estate planning in the context of a second marriage. Each situation is unique and requires the skilled counsel that only an estate planning lawyer with family law experience can provide.

CHAPTER 24

Planning for Same-Sex Marriages and/or Couples Living Together

What's black and brown and looks good on an attorney?

Jamie Hargrove

A doberman pinscher.

There are some unique planning issues when your significant other is not your legally recognized spouse. This applies not only to same-sex couples, but also to heterosexual couples living together. In some situations for a legally married couple, state statutes, appropriately executed beneficiary designations and properly titled accounts and real property may effectively get your assets to your spouse if you don't have a Last Will and Testament. This is more likely if you do not have children. However, unless you are legally married and residing in a state that recognizes your marriage, most states are not going to do anything to protect your partner. This makes a will even more important for unmarried couples.

If you are a same-sex couple married under the laws of your particular state, I suggest you don't leave anything to chance. While state laws are changing, the case-law history is likely going to create numerous conflicts and questions. Prepare and execute your will (and other documents such as power of attorney and healthcare directives) so you don't have to worry about what the state law has to say, at least as to how your estate is distributed and who is to make your important decisions.

Some unmarried couples may be sensitive about the "public" nature of their information during the handling of their estates. If that is true for you, it will be important to set up an estate plan using a living trust to help avoid the public nature of probate.

One area that can be troublesome for unmarried couples is federal and state inheritance and estate taxation. For same-sex couples are validly married and living in a state that legally recognizes their marriage, they are now given the same rights and benefits as traditionally married couples. For couples who are not legally married, however, there can be a huge tax problem for the survivor. For these couples, there is no "marital deduction" for inheritance and estate tax purposes. The federal estate tax system is designed to allow a married couple to defer their estate tax liability, if any, until the time of the second person's death. If the couple is unmarried, that very significant benefit is lost. There simply is no protection for the unmarried, surviving partner from a death tax standpoint.

Also, while many states have eliminated state inheritance or state estate taxes for certain family members, many only exempt a beneficiary from the tax if he or she is of a certain relationship to the decedent. Thus, a surviving "non-family member" (or unmarried partner) can get hit with some pretty hefty taxes. Unmarried couples will want to consider planning to avoid those taxes, or at least to anticipate them.

End of Lawyers? Probably not. For the protection of an unmarried partner, it is best to consult with a trained estate planning attorney to navigate potential conflicts and pitfalls.

CHAPTER 25

Pet Trusts: Don't Forget to Take Care of Fido

*What's the difference between
God and a lawyer?*

Jamie Hargrove

God does not think he is a lawyer!

It is estimated that there are approximately 78.2 million dogs and 86.4 million cats owned in the United States alone. Pet ownership is a significant part of American culture. For some, a pet is just a pet. For many others, however, a pet is an integral part of the family. While the importance of a pet and its care can be a priority for any individual or family situation, if there are no children at home, a pet can take on a much greater significance.

Because of our affection for our pets, it is only just that we plan for their care upon our death or disability. You need to designate who will care for your pet, as well as a backup person if your first choice is unwilling or unable to do so. Another important consideration is the financial aspect of pet ownership. You may leave your estate to kids and grandkids but choose a close friend or neighbor to care for your pet because that person is more affectionate toward your pet than your family. Are you going to saddle your friend or neighbor with the ongoing costs of pet care with no compensation or coverage for pet expenses? Pet ownership is not inexpensive, and certainly the last thing you want is someone to skimp on your pet's care.

In my opinion, the best way to protect your pet is with a combination of a pet trust and a pet power of attorney.

First, let's discuss the pet power of attorney. This is simply a document that authorizes someone on your behalf to take care of your pet should you become disabled. While most of us think about the care of our pets after we die, it is equally important to think about the pet's care during periods of disability.

The pet power of attorney should name an individual or individuals, as well as successors, to care for the pet during your disability. People's situations change, so someone you choose today may find himself in a situation where the responsibility of one or more pets would be a significant inconvenience, or even an impossibility. The other function of a pet power of attorney is to make it clear that your money can be utilized for the pet's care.

In addition to a general power of attorney, you need to incorporate provisions for the healthcare and end-of-life decisions for your pet. For my individual clients, I generally recommend separating the general power of attorney from the healthcare power of attorney. However, in pet care situations, we suggest combining those into a single document.

While a pet power of attorney would cease to be effective upon your death, a pet trust is generally designed to take effect at your death. If you are planning to establish a pet trust, I strongly encourage you to also set up a good pet health insurance program. You can always provide in your pet trust that such a policy be purchased at the time of your death, and provide the necessary funds for such a purchase. The problem, however, is that you can't know whether your pet will qualify for insurance at that time. If the pet is already sick or has significant health issues, it may not qualify for insurance. For this reason, I encourage clients to seriously consider putting pet insurance in place immediately. Even if you set up a bare-bones policy today, many companies will allow the policy to be upgraded later without any insurability issues.

The pet trust, like a pet care power of attorney during your lifetime, will dictate who is to care for your pet after you are deceased. Also like a power of attorney, it will name successor individuals to serve in such capacity. A pet trust, however, will also segregate funds from your estate to provide for your pets. If you have pet health insurance, the amount of funds that need to be segregated are much more easily calculated than if you do not have pet health insurance. The funds in the pet trust can generally remain available for a pet's lifetime, or up to 21 years. More and more states are passing legislation to specifically allow for pet trusts. However, just because a state has not specifically provided legislative authority for a pet trust does not mean that you cannot create one. In such states, the trust will generally be restricted to a 21-year time period, with possible other restrictions. However, even if you are living in a state with no pet trust legislation, you can still establish a trust. In some situations, it may be advisable to establish the pet trust in a state other than the one in which you live. Some jurisdictions will allow for that.

A pet trust can be set up as a standalone trust, which means its sole use and purpose is for the benefit of a pet. Such a trust can also be established as a sub-trust within other trust planning. If you are already setting up a living trust, family protection trust or other trust for your family, you could certainly incorporate a pet trust into those documents.

You can also set up a pet trust under a Last Will and Testament. The concern there, however, is that if there is no specific legislation dealing with a pet trust in your state, there will likely be some issues about the required reporting and administrative responsibilities in local probate court. Even in states where there is legislation, some court oversight is still likely for the trust. However, if a pet trust is set up as a separate trust or a sub-trust (i.e., not under your will), the probate court will not have any jurisdiction over it, which will make its administration much simpler, smoother and easier.

End of Lawyers? Probably not. Lawyers will continue to be in demand in this area of estate planning. To ensure your pet is cared for in the event of your disability or death, use a trained attorney to set up the provisions of a pet power of attorney or pet trust. Because legislation varies from state to state, legal experience is often needed. While my company provides state-specific pet trusts, online legal forms services do not provide comprehensive coverage for this important type of planning.

CHAPTER 26

Gun Trusts:
Second Amendment Trust

Where can you find a good lawyer?

At the city morgue.

Gun Trusts: Second Amendment Trust | 195

I noted in an earlier chapter that some people believe everyone needs a living trust. Some have also argued that anyone who owns a gun needs a gun trust. Really? You may own a gun but have never heard of a gun trust. That certainly wouldn't be unusual. A gun trust is not something your grandfather or father talked about because they have only been around for a relatively short time.

I would agree that everyone who owns a gun should consider a gun trust. Not everyone will need one, but if you are a serious gun owner, you'll want to pay attention to the benefits a gun trust can offer. To many, the gun trust is a loophole in the government's attempt to regulate gun owners and their rights to possess, share and transfer guns.

If you own any weapon, or more importantly, if you own or intend to purchase a Title II firearm, you probably need a gun trust. Examples of Title II firearms are:

- Fully automatic guns
- Silencers
- Short-barreled ("sawed-off") shotguns and rifles
- Explosive devices
- And a host of other weapons that may be less likely to be found in your gun cabinet.

Before I give you the four primary reasons why you may want to consider a gun trust, let me give you a little background. The federal government started regulating firearms with the National Firearms Act of 1934. In 1968, the Gun Control Act was passed, which includes Title II. It put in place strict guidelines for the ownership, transfer and possession of Title II firearms.

If you break the rules, you may be subject to fines of as much as $250,000 and be imprisoned for up to 10 years. This is serious stuff! One of the rules for Title II firearms is that only manufacturers, makers and importers are allowed to register

Jamie Hargrove

firearms. That means that if you own a Title II firearm and you're not a manufacturer, maker or importer, and your gun is not registered, you're in trouble — big trouble. Your only "out" is to immediately contact the Bureau of Alcohol, Tobacco, Firearms and Explosives (ATF) and turn over your firearm. No, they are not going to register it for you. No, they're not going to hold onto or store your firearm. They are going to dispose of it. The good news is that if you have a good explanation for why you have the firearm, and you are the one who brings it to their attention, you probably won't be fined or go to jail.

When the legislation was passed, "owner" was defined to include not only individuals but also corporations and trusts. Because trusts have fewer public reporting and registration requirements than corporations, trusts have developed as the "entity of choice" to own guns, and certainly to own Title II firearms.

One of the complexities in this area is that it's not just the federal government that regulates firearms. There are also state regulations, and while there are some consistent statutory themes, every state has its own unique approach to regulating the acquisition, use and transfer of firearms.

A gun trust is not like any other trust discussed in this book. It is a very unique, special-purpose trust. A gun trust should not be designed to hold anything other than guns. That's not a legislative requirement, but a practical requirement of how gun trusts work. That means that simply adding another paragraph or two to your living trust is not going to convert it into a gun trust that can legally acquire and own a Title II firearm.

One example of the difference between a gun trust and virtually any other trust is that the trustee has the right to use the firearms owned by the trust. In virtually every other trust, the trustee simply maintains and manages assets for the use and benefit of the beneficiary. With a gun trust, it is the trustee who gets the opportunity to use the firearm, not the beneficiary. In a gun trust, the beneficiary is the person who ultimately will end up with any non-Title II firearms and/or proceeds from the sale of firearms at the time the trust terminates, if ever.

For example, you cannot create a gun trust, have your five children as beneficiaries with you as trustee and expect all five of your children to have free use of the Title II firearms. That is not the loophole I'm talking about. Could you have all five of your children be co-trustees of the trust and hence have access to the Title II firearms owned by the trust? Yes, but the trust needs to be carefully designed to allow for such a large group of trustees. I should also point out that, in a gun trust, co-trustees are jointly and severally liable for each other. That means that if there are five children and one of them goes off the deep end and does something stupid with a Title II firearm, all five children may end up getting fined, going to jail or both. Didn't I tell you this was serious stuff?

Gun trusts can come from several different sources. More and more gun dealers are making a trust form available. While I have not researched the quality or effectiveness of the gun trust forms used by dealers, experts caution against using a gun dealer's forms. A lot of those forms look more like a living trust (described in Chapter 4) rather than a customized gun trust designed to avoid significant penalties and keep you out of jail. There are, of course, attorneys who specialize in this area. However, this specialty practice is still not common. If you are going to hire an attorney, you may need to search a bit to find someone who really understands the intricacies of gun trust laws. There are also online companies that offer state-by-state gun trust products. My own company, NetLaw, is one such company that is working to add gun trusts to its online set of estate planning documents and will be recruiting attorneys who have expertise in this area as part of its resource network.

The four benefits that gun trusts are known for are:

1. <u>Multiple gun ownership.</u> As a general rule, a firearm can only be owned by one individual. If the firearm is a Title II firearm, it can be used only by that particular individual. As mentioned above, a gun trust allows such use to be expanded to multiple individuals. The multiple individuals will be the trustees of the trust.

2. <u>Easier registration.</u> It is this benefit that has a lot of people up in arms (excuse the pun). As an individual, in order to register a Title II firearm, you must be fingerprinted, undergo a background check and get local law enforcement's approval. With a gun trust, that's not the case. Why? Well, when the legislation was passed, it made sense that trusts or corporations did not have fingerprints, nor did these types of entities/structures have criminal records. Consequently, there was no need to capture a fingerprint or a background check.

   Legislators could have required that anyone serving as the trustee would have to go through the fingerprinting and background check. I'm clueless as to why they didn't require that. Yes, this is a loophole, and it's a potential way for bad people to get their hands on weapons for bad purposes.

   I'm told that any reputable gun dealer or manufacturer will require background checks and fingerprinting any time he sells firearms. That doesn't mean that there are not some dealers out there who don't do this, and therefore run the risk of putting weapons in the hands of criminals.

3. <u>Ease of transfer.</u> A transfer for the purposes of federal, and most state, laws is going to occur when

the trust terminates and distributes its assets to a beneficiary. At that point, you have the same transfer rules that are applicable to any individual ownership.

The beauty of a gun trust, however, is that you effectively can make a transfer within the gun trust simply by changing the trustees of the trust. If the trust is set up pursuant to perpetual trust statutes in a state that has those kinds of statutes, the firearms can be effectively transferred from individual to individual and generation to generation via trustee appointment and never again registered.

4. <u>Probate avoidance.</u> There are some similarities between a gun trust and a living trust. A living trust can be used to avoid probate via assets owned by the living trust at the time of a person's death. The same applies with a gun trust. With Title II firearms, avoiding probate becomes a much more critical issue.

When someone dies, federal law provides that the executor or personal representative for that person's estate becomes responsible and liable for the oversight and control of the Title II firearms. Such personal representative must take possession, and during the time held by the representative, no one else has the right to possess the Title II firearms. Such personal representative will have liability (again, fines and potential imprisonment) if he or she does not strictly control the firearms.

Depending on the firearms, as well as the age, identity and criminal background of the executor and the relevant beneficiary of the estate, it is possible that a particular Title II firearm cannot be retained by the executor or transferred to a designated beneficiary because that particular individual is not otherwise qualified to own such firearm. If either is true, the firearm will have to be turned over to the authorities to be disposed of.

With a gun trust, the death of the person setting up the trust, or of a trustee, does not trigger the termination of the trust unless the trust specifically provides for such termination. Generally, a properly designed trust is not going to provide for such automatic termination. If there is no trust termination, there is no need for re-registration at the person's death.

In some respects, a gun trust is almost too good to be true. And as we all know, if something seems too good to be true, it probably has issues. The real problem with gun trusts is whether the U.S. Congress will effectively legislate them out of existence. If this happens, many believe that any existing gun trusts will be grandfathered. While no one can be certain, history shows that in every other kind of trust situation, Congress has tended to grandfather trusts that are irrevocable and already in place at the time the legislation is either passed or proposed.

Keep in mind, "confiscation" is a political third rail. While it is highly unlikely that there would be new laws allowing our government broad rights to confiscate our firearms, there is another approach. If the government merely prohibits the transfer of a firearm, Title II or not, it has effectively created a "quieter" approach to confiscation. If, in the future, an estate can't legally transfer a firearm, it will most likely be forced to surrender it to the authorities. Thus, avoiding future transfers via use of a trust may assist in avoiding the equivalent of confiscation.

If the information in this chapter is applicable to your situation and you do not have a gun trust, or if your current trust is not sophisticated enough to accomplish all of your goals, I recommend you don't wait to establish a gun trust.

End of Lawyers? Possibly. Even though laws vary from state to state and create a lot of complexity, overall gun trusts are a pretty good scenario for online planning. Your chances of finding an online site that can deliver the kind of gun trust you need is probably pretty good.

CHARITY

CHAPTER 27

Charitable Trusts

What is the difference between a female lawyer and a pitbull?

Jamie Hargrove

Lipstick.

THE END of LAWYERS: *Thank Goodness!*

Entire books have been written on charitable estate planning. So rather than try to cover this extensive topic here, I'll focus on charitable trusts. Of course, there are numerous types of charitable trusts. For those of you who are charitably inclined, you should explore the income tax benefits that many of these trusts provide with your accountant. This chapter will focus only on charitable remainder trusts (CRT), which tend to be the most commonly used.

A CRT can be designed in a number of ways. Your first decision lies in whether to create an "annuity trust" (charitable reminder annuity trust, or CRAT) or a "unitrust" (charitable remainder unitrust, or CRUT).

The term "annuity"[6] is not a reference to commercial annuity, which is an investment product sold by financial institutions. Instead, it is a reference to the type of payment that the CRT will make to its individual beneficiaries. Like some commercial annuities, the payment from a CRAT is a fixed payment that, once calculated (upon creation of the trust), does not change from year to year. Because the fixed payment is similar to many payments paid out of commercial annuities, the term "annuity" in this case is sometimes confused with the commercial product. However, the term is simply adopted because of the nature of payments made out of the trust. A CRAT can also be structured to pay out funds for a fixed amount of time, such as 20 years, regardless of how long the beneficiary lives.

A CRT generally benefits the person who establishes the trust. It can also benefit other individuals, such as a spouse and children. A CRT can be for a term of years (i.e., 15 years) or can span the life of one or more beneficiaries.

For example, if a husband and wife set up a CRT, they often will retain an income stream from it for their joint lives, and then for the survivor's lifetime. During such lifetimes, monthly, quarterly or annual payments will be made from the CRT. After

---

6 An annuity is a continuing payment with a fixed total amount.

the beneficiaries' deaths, the assets remaining in the CRT are transferred to the trust's chosen charity or charities.

In very brief terms, here is a comparison between the two types of CRTs:

- **CRAT:** A CRAT provides for a fixed payment each year to individual beneficiaries. The percentage rate for the trust (discussed below) is used at the time of the initial funding to determine a fixed payment for the remaining lifetime of the beneficiaries (or a term of years). The payment will not increase or decrease over the lifetime of the beneficiaries. The advantage of this type of trust is that it provides certainty in terms of annual payments. The disadvantage is that if the assets in the CRAT continually increase in value, the lifetime beneficiaries will not be able to take advantage of the possible increasing payment a CRUT would provide. For example, a $1,000 per month payment today is not going to have the same purchasing power as a $1,000 per month payment in 20 years (assuming the beneficiary is still alive in 20 years).

- **CRUT:** The CRUT re-calculates the payment to the beneficiary each year. The percentage rate for the trust (again, discussed below) is used at the time of the initial funding to calculate the first year's payment(s). Each year thereafter, the percentage rate is used to calculate a new payment amount based on the CRUT's value at that time. If the market value of the CRUT has gone up, then the payment to the life beneficiary for the next year will increase. Likewise, if the value of the CRUT assets has dropped from the previous year's valuation, the payment to the life beneficiary for the next year will decrease. Each year, therefore, the payment will increase or decrease based on the value of the assets held in the CRUT. The advantage of this trust is that if the assets in the CRUT continually increase in value, the life beneficiary's payment will also increase. This will negate inflationary concerns of having a fixed payment. The disadvantage of this type of trust is that the certainty of a guaranteed fixed payment (as long as there are trust assets to pay it) is lost. This is particularly problematic if the value of the CRUT continually drops in value.

EXAMPLE:

Assumptions:

- Mrs. Jones has a $300,000 piece of commercial real estate that she intends to sell.

- Her income tax basis in the property is $100,000, which means that when she sells the property, she will have a $200,000 taxable gain ($300,000 sale - $100,000 tax basis).

- She wants to avoid the $60,000+ in state and federal capital gains taxes she is going to have to pay when she sells her property.

- Mrs. Jones no longer wants to own real estate, so a Section 1031 like-kind exchange[7] of her property for another property is not an option.

Establishment of a CRT:

- Mrs. Jones sets up a CRT. The charity that she wants to eventually benefit from the CRT will be the trustee.

---

7 Section 1031 of the Internal Revenue Code governs like-kind exchanges. For people who do a lot of property exchanges, they might refer to them as "Section 1031 Exchanges." A Section 1031 Exchange allows for capital gains taxes to be deferred on the sale of property, provided the money received is reinvested in similar (or "like kind") property within a certain time period.

Note: not all states will allow a charity to serve as a trustee of a CRT.

- The CRT provides Mrs. Jones a certain return from the trust. She wants the target percentage for the trust to be 6%. Her annual payment will depend on the type of trust she sets up:
  - **CRAT:** The "annuity" trust will give Mrs. Jones a fixed payment based on 6% of the initial value of the trust. The payment to Mrs. Jones thereafter will be fixed at the same amount. The payment will not increase or decrease.
  - **CRUT:** The "unitrust" approach gives Mrs. Jones the same 6%, except her payment is recalculated each year. So the first year, the payment to Mrs. Jones is the same whether she sets up CRAT or a CRUT. Since the CRUT recalculates each year, if the value of the CRT goes up or down, then the payment to Mrs. Jones will be greater or lesser than what it would have been using a CRAT.

Gift of property to CRT then sale:

- Mrs. Jones will deed her property to her new CRT.
- The CRT will then enter into a contract for the sale of the property.
- The CRT will sell the property.

Result:

- Because the CRT is a "charitable" trust, there is no gain on the sale of the property, leaving 100% of the proceeds from the sale to be reinvested by the CRT and used to generate the annual payment to Mrs. Jones.

Wealth Replacement Trust:

- With a lot of CRT planning situations, the motivation for planning may ***not*** be charitable intentions. In some cases, therefore, life insurance may be used to create a pool of cash to go to the donor's family (i.e., Mrs. Jones' family) in "replacement" of the asset given away to charity through the CRT.

- The theory of this type of planning, if there is little or no charitable intent, is that the individual beneficiary can pay for the insurance solely from the larger payment generated by the additional capital, which was made available when income taxes were avoided on the sale. Of course, this is directly impacted by the insurability of the donor — Mrs. Jones in this case.

- Often, the "replacement" life insurance is placed in an irrevocable life insurance trust, sometimes referred to as a "wealth replacement trust."

The above is an over-simplification of charitable planning using one type of trust. Some other considerations in this type of planning may include:

- If the gift is a transfer of real estate, there are rules that will address issues related to mortgaged real estate. The presence of debt, possible satisfaction of such debt or the donor's release of liability from such debt can significantly impact the tax advantages of the planning.

- The CRT can have more than one life beneficiary. For example, the trust can provide an income interest for the joint and survivor lives of a husband and wife. Also, in some cases the trust can continue to make distributions to children (depending on their ages) before it eventually distributes its assets to the charity.

- Real estate should not be under a binding sales contract before it is transferred to the CRT. Any binding agreements relating to the sale should only be entered into after the transfer.

- It should be noted that the CRT can allow for the charity's name to be changed and can also name multiple charities. A donor-advised fund at a community foundation can also be named as a beneficiary.

End of Lawyers? No, lawyers are safe here. Because of the complex tax rules that can play into charitable trust planning, a lawyer should always be at the table to advise consumers in this important area.

CHAPTER 28

The Family Foundation: Private Foundations and Donor-Advised Funds

What's the difference between a good lawyer and a bad lawyer?

*A bad lawyer
can let a case drag out for several years.*

*A good lawyer
can make it last even longer.*

One of my greatest joys in the practice of law is watching my clients become involved in matters that are more about others and less about themselves. It is always exciting to see folks who have a passion for helping their communities, whether that passion goes toward secular causes or religious ones. Something special happens in an individual when he turns his focus from accumulating to giving, particularly when the giving is to those less fortunate.

My happiest clients are not the clients who make the most money. But I'm sure you knew that! My most content clients are also not my poorest clients. My happiest clients are poor, wealthy and everything in between, but more importantly, they are people whose main focus points away from themselves and shines toward others. This means more than simply writing a check — it means showing a true passion for the causes they support.

If your passion is only for the next deal, the next dollar or the next paycheck, then I suspect life will come up short in meeting your expectations. For this reason, I will continue to encourage my clients and readers like you to think and pray about where you can use not only your checkbook, but your talents, your gifts, your background and your experience to make a difference in the lives of those in need.

One way to formalize this passion is to establish a donor-advised fund with a community foundation or similar organization. I established an online donor-advised fund with the National Christian Foundation many years ago. It has been instrumental in helping my family manage our giving, as well as provide encouragement to the organizations we avidly support.

You can establish donor-advised funds with most national religious organizations. Whether it be Christian, Jewish, Muslim or others, there are many opportunities to become involved in very solid organizations that facilitate your charitable giving. Donor-advised funds, however, are not just part of religious foundations. Local community foundations are a key resource in many cities across the country as well.

The Community Foundation of Louisville, Kentucky, where I live, is undoubtedly one of the best in the country. While community foundations were once found only in large cities, they are now popping up in smaller communities. Many smaller community foundations might also be affiliated in some way with a community foundation in a larger city.

These organizations are a tremendous resource for people who want to find creative ways to give or simply manage their routine giving. Rather than my wife and I having to make quick decisions on where we want extra funds beyond our church tithe to go at the end of the year, we can simply direct those extra dollars to our donor-advised fund. Then, over the coming weeks, months and years, we will decide how that money is distributed to the organizations we support. We get our immediate charitable deduction for income tax purposes, but without having to quickly decide which organization we want the funds to benefit. For many people, a donor-advised fund also serves as an alternative to a private foundation.

Community foundations, larger religious foundations and many larger universities are an excellent resource for complex tax and charitable planning. Avoiding income tax on the sale of a business or a real estate investment can be carefully planned with the help and expertise of many of these organizations.

For the right situation, a private foundation can be a rewarding pursuit. Having your own charitable organization to manage and operate can be very fulfilling. If your foundation will encourage others to donate to its causes, host events or activities and will be substantial in nature, then a family foundation may be the best option. If you can get broad support from other donors, you may even be able to qualify as a public charity.

Some of the roadblocks you may encounter with

establishing a private family foundation may be:

- Up-front, as well as ongoing, costs can be significant. In contrast, there is no cost either to establish a donor-advised fund or to maintain it from year to year.

- IRS reporting can be complex and time-consuming. You will not only have to file annual tax returns, you will continuously need to monitor the organization's operations to ensure that it is not conflicting with IRS rules and regulations. The IRS monitors family foundations very closely. There is a lot of abuse in this area, and consequently the IRS spends a lot of time and effort to make sure that the foundation is in compliance. A private foundation is not a magic, tax-saving tool that will allow you to simply convert taxable dollars into tax-free funds. It has tax benefits, for sure, but these don't come without a lot of work.

- Day-to-day management is an important consideration. When you create a private foundation, someone will have to run this separate, legal entity. You'll also need a succession plan in place, and there is no guarantee that other family members will have the same passion for your family foundation as you do. Too often, the passion of a family foundation dies with its leader.

- There are also some income tax deduction limitations with family foundations versus public charities. As one example, with a family foundation, your deduction for appreciated assets such as marketable securities may be limited to your cost basis rather than their current fair market value. A deduction based on the tax basis in the asset (instead of its current fair market value) can be a significant disadvantage of a private foundation.

One of the advantages of making charitable gifts through a donor-advised fund rather than establishing a private foundation is the added tax benefits. For example, some of my clients handle their giving through their donor-advised fund, using a transfer of low-basis marketable securities. The community foundation managing the fund sells the low-basis securities without any income tax consequences. The donor gets the full 100% charitable deduction based on the fair market value of the securities and does not have to report the gain on sale. If it was a donated stock that the donor otherwise would have kept, the donor can simply repurchase the stock using cash he or she would have otherwise used to make the gift to charity. The difference, of course, is that the donor would then have a higher basis in the stock that he or she has just purchased. Bottom line, if you are making lots of charitable gifts and you also have a large block of low-basis marketable securities, you should give serious consideration to using a donor-advised fund and look into a plan for giving away stock, not cash.

Gifts of real estate and business interests also provide an attractive income tax opportunity. When it comes to mortgaged property or gifts of stock or membership units in a closely held company, there can be lots of tax complications. Large foundations can be a great resource in this area.

The table below includes some of the differences between a family foundation and a donor-advised fund within a community foundation or similar organization. I have also included on the table comparisons to a "supporting organization."

A "supporting organization" is one that is sponsored by a community foundation or similar public charity. A supporting organization offers the best of both worlds. It gives you the tax benefits of a public charity yet also allows you to have your own private entity. The public charity ultimately has control and oversight over your family foundation, but in many situations, it's not day-to-day oversight. It allows you to basically operate as an independent family foundation as long as you meet the requirements of the IRS and of the sponsoring organization. There are added costs to this approach but, depending on your circumstances, they may be worth the added expense.

PRIVATE FOUNDATIONS VS. SUPPORTING ORGANIZATIONS VS. COMMUNITY FOUNDATIONS		
PRIVATE ("FAMILY") FOUNDATIONS	SUPPORTING ORGANIZATIONS	COMMUNITY FOUNDATIONS
DONOR CONTROL:		
Donor control is permitted.	Donor control is less than that of a private foundation. The donor can recommend grants and investment management.	Control is limited. Through a donor-advised fund, the donor can make non-binding suggestions to the community foundation about how, where and when funds should be spent, but the community foundation is the owner of the funds and can decline to follow the donor's suggestions.

PRIVATE FOUNDATIONS VS. SUPPORTING ORGANIZATIONS VS. COMMUNITY FOUNDATIONS

PRIVATE ("FAMILY") FOUNDATIONS	SUPPORTING ORGANIZATIONS	COMMUNITY FOUNDATIONS
INCOME TAX CONSEQUENCES (Cash and Nonappreciated Property):		
For gifts of cash, an income tax deduction, limited to 30% of the donor's adjusted gross income is allowed. Amounts not currently deductible can be carried forward five years.	The donor can deduct up to 50% of adjusted gross income for gifts of cash or other nonappreciated property to a supporting organization. Amounts not deductible in the year of contribution can be carried forward for five years.	The donor can deduct up to 50% of adjusted gross income for gifts of cash or other nonappreciated property to a community foundation. Amounts not deductible in the year of contribution can be carried forward for five years.
INCOME TAX CONSEQUENCES (Long-Term Appreciated Property):		
For gifts of long-term capital gain property, the donor can deduct up to 20% of adjusted gross income (AGI). Amounts not currently deductible can be carried forward five years.	For gifts of long-term capital gain property, the donor can deduct up to 30% of adjusted gross income (AGI). Amounts not currently deductible can be carried forward five years.	The donor can deduct up to 50% of adjusted gross income for gifts of cash or other nonappreciated property and up to 30% of AGI for gifts of long-term capital gain property. Amounts not deductible in the year of contribution can be carried forward for five years.

PRIVATE FOUNDATIONS VS. SUPPORTING ORGANIZATIONS VS. COMMUNITY FOUNDATIONS

PRIVATE ("FAMILY") FOUNDATIONS	SUPPORTING ORGANIZATIONS	COMMUNITY FOUNDATIONS
INCOME TAX CONSEQUENCES (All Other Appreciated Property):		
For gifts of all other appreciated property, including appreciated stock, the donor may only deduct the income tax basis (generally the cost) of the contributed property. The deduction is limited to 20% of AGI.	100% of the fair market value of the appreciated property, including capital gain, is deductible up to 30% of the donor's AGI.	100% of the fair market value of the appreciated property, including capital gain, is deductible up to 30% of the donor's AGI.
EXCISE TAX ON INVESTMENT INCOME:		
A 2% excise tax is imposed on the net investment income of the private foundation, including interests, dividends, rents, royalties, long- and short-term capital gains. The tax may be reduced to 1% if the private foundation donates a sufficient amount to qualified charities.	No excise tax on investment income is imposed.	No excise tax on investment income is imposed.

PRIVATE FOUNDATIONS VS. SUPPORTING ORGANIZATIONS VS. COMMUNITY FOUNDATIONS		
PRIVATE ("FAMILY") FOUNDATIONS	**SUPPORTING ORGANIZATIONS**	**COMMUNITY FOUNDATIONS**
PAY-OUT REQUIREMENTS		
Whether or not the foundation earns such an amount, approximately 5% of the fair market value of the foundation's net investment assets must be distributed for charitable purposes each year.	There are no minimum payout requirements imposed on supporting organizations; therefore, they have more flexibility in accepting gifts of undeveloped real estate and other assets that currently produce little or no yield but are being retained for future yield.	There are no minimum payout requirements imposed on community foundations; therefore, they have more flexibility in accepting gifts of undeveloped real estate and other assets that currently produce little or no yield but are being retained for future yield.

PRIVATE FOUNDATIONS VS. SUPPORTING ORGANIZATIONS VS. COMMUNITY FOUNDATIONS

PRIVATE ("FAMILY") FOUNDATIONS	SUPPORTING ORGANIZATIONS	COMMUNITY FOUNDATIONS
SELF-DEALING:		
Self-dealing (economic activities such as a sale or lease of property or the furnishing of goods or services) between a private foundation and those who manage, control or make large gifts to the private foundation and persons and corporations closely related to them ("disqualified persons") are strictly regulated. Significant excise tax is imposed on self-dealing transactions. These rules apply without regard to whether the foundation is better off as a result of such dealings.	Subject to the same self-dealing and excess business holdings as a private foundation.	These regulations do not apply, and a community foundation can do business with its contributors and managers and engage in transactions that are advantageous to the foundation.
HIGH-RISK INVESTMENTS:		
A private foundation cannot invest its funds in ways that could jeopardize the foundation's ability to carry out its charitable purposes. Risky investments can be subject to federal excise tax.	A supporting organization cannot invest its funds in ways that could jeopardize the foundation's ability to carry out its charitable purposes. Risky investments can be subject to federal excise tax.	No federal investment requirements are imposed, but state fiduciary duties may be similar.

PRIVATE FOUNDATIONS VS. SUPPORTING ORGANIZATIONS VS. COMMUNITY FOUNDATIONS		
PRIVATE ("FAMILY") FOUNDATIONS	SUPPORTING ORGANIZATIONS	COMMUNITY FOUNDATIONS
EXCESS BUSINESS HOLDINGS:		
In order to prevent a private foundation, its contributors or managers from having controlling ownership of a business, the foundation and its disqualified persons combined may not hold more than 20% of the equity interest in a business that is owned by the foundation.	Generally, a supporting organization is not subject to the private foundation excise tax penalties on self-dealing or excess business holdings.	These regulations do not apply, so the community foundation may hold unlimited business interests.

End of Lawyers? Maybe. A factor that may determine whether a family should set up a foundation versus a donor-advised fund is that one requires an attorney (family foundation), while the other does not (donor-advised fund). While there may be online document services that advocate for the establishment of a family foundation without the use of an attorney, that is only because it serves their end purposes. My advice is, if you want to set up a family foundation, make sure you put together a team that includes an experienced lawyer, CPA and financial advisors and possibly even the charity or charities you hope to benefit from your new organization. A team approach will help you achieve the best results.

PLANNING FOR
THE FAMILY BUSINESS

CHAPTER 29

Business Succession Planning

Why won't sharks attack lawyers?

Jamie Hargrove

Professional courtesy.

There is nothing more important for a business than its business succession plan. Whether you have family members directly involved in your business or not, planning for its future succession is essential. The sooner, the better.

Unfortunately, as important as succession planning is to the longevity of any business, it is probably the topic least likely to be addressed by a business owner. Too often, a business owner will view a buy-sell agreement as his or her succession plan. While a buy-sell agreement[8] may be an integral component of a succession plan, it is not, in and of itself, a succession plan.

Some of the questions a business succession plan will address are:

- When the owner or owners die or become disabled, who will operate the business? A family member active in the business, or a non-related key employee? Or will the business simply have to be sold because there is no one to step in and take over?

- If you have targeted a key employee to eventually run the business, what will that look like? Will the key employee have ownership in the family business? If so, how much? How much control will the key employee be given?

- What is the plan if the key employee leaves the company?

- What incentives and "golden handcuffs" have you put in place to better ensure that your key employee does not leave?

- If the plan is simply to sell the business upon the death or disability of the owner or owners, what is

---

8 A buy-sell agreement (sometimes called a shareholders agreement for corporations) is an agreement among the owners of the company. The agreement usually outlines the rights surviving owners will have to purchase a deceased owner's ownership interest (usually stock for corporations). The agreement may also address disposition of ownership interests upon the disability of an owner and possibly other issues.

being done now to ready the business for the eventual sale? Have you met with professional advisors who handle these types of business transactions in your industry to determine how to ready your company for a sale in terms of operations and financial considerations? Many professionals advise that you should have your company ready to sell at all times. Since you do not know when death or disability can occur, the company may need to be sold in the short term instead of well into the future. If you ready your company for a sale now, that doesn't mean you have to sell. Instead, your family is better situated if the unexpected happens. Your family does not have to risk losing a significant portion of the value of the company that you have worked so hard to create.

The goal for some business owners is to gradually transition into retirement. That doesn't just happen. It involves the same type of succession planning as the transition of leadership resulting from death or disability of the owner. The difference, of course, is that the owner will still be around in retirement or partial retirement. He or she may be available as a consultant or want to retain some income from the business.

Business owners too often view themselves as invincible. They can't imagine they will ever have a drop in energy or ability. Age and unexpected illness, however, can slow us down. Having a plan for a key person or a team of employees to run the company if the owner has to take some time off (even temporarily) is essential. A good trial would be to take a vacation. You might be surprised to learn how many business owners never take a vacation day. Just not enough time! A vacation can allow a business owner to test his or her newer, younger leadership while he or she is still around to "clean up," if need be.

I said earlier that a buy-sell agreement may be some

business owners' only evidence of a business succession plan. Many buy-sell agreements deal with the death of the owner. Sometimes they deal with disability or other challenges (e.g., bankruptcy, divorce or retirement). Too often, however, the focus is only on the owner's death. Even if the buy-sell deals with possible lifetime transfers, those plans are usually not as well thought out as the details related to a transfer upon death. Consequently, if there is a lifetime transfer as a result of disability, retirement, divorce or bankruptcy, the agreement could have some unexpected outcomes.

While I do not want to discourage a business owner from having a buy-sell agreement, I do want to encourage him or her to rethink the terms and give more attention to the various "what ifs" that can happen.

A buy-sell agreement can become dated very quickly. Many times, there will be a value placed on the owner's stock, and within a few years the value is out of date. This can mean the owner's family gets less fair market value for the owner's interest in the business. Some agreements require an annual update. But even if an annual update is not completed (many times they aren't), the agreement should address a possible change in the value of the owner's portion of the company.

When dealing with a buy-sell agreement, there are numerous key issues that will need to be addressed. One of the most important is cash flow and how the business owner is going to get paid for his or her ownership interest in the business. One of the reasons the buy-sell agreement can work so well when it addresses the death of the owner is that the cash needed to buy the owner out can be provided by a life insurance policy on the owner. For other possible triggering events, life insurance is not necessarily going to cover the cash needs of a buy-out.

Using the guidance I have provided here, I suggest that you put your business succession plan in writing. Do it with the goal of setting aside at least a day each year to review and update the plan. If you don't have the discipline or lack the expertise, hire someone to do it for you. That may be a corporate attorney. More often, it will be a trained financial or business advisor who specializes in business succession planning.

To do it justice, you want to create a team to work on your business succession plan. Include your CPA, your business lawyer, your insurance and financial advisor(s) and an outside consultant if you choose to engage one.

As you go through your business succession planning, involve any family members who may be impacted by the end result. That could include your spouse and your adult children. It may not include your sons-in-law or daughters-in-law, unless they are involved in the business.

When family is brought into the discussion, you should not feel obligated to open up every aspect of your business and succession plan. I have clients who keep their adult children mostly in the dark about their business and only share the big picture of who will ultimately take over for the owner. However, it is generally better if the adult children get an opportunity to ask their parent/owner questions before the owner becomes mentally disabled or deceased. Otherwise, they can only speculate on why and how decisions were made.

I hear all the time from clients that "my spouse really doesn't care" or "my kids really aren't interested." Well, that may be the case while you are running things. But take you out of the picture, and I can assure you they will care. Push them to be interested now and solicit their input. You are the boss. You are in control. There is no harm in asking what they think. You will still decide what to do with that input, if anything.

End of Lawyers? No. If there is ever a need for a well-equipped business, tax and estate planning lawyer, this is it. Business succession planning for a family-owned or other closely held business is critical. While the attorney engaged should be competent in several key areas, he or she ideally also will be wired into some online systems and processes that will make the delivery of those services much more efficient. I do see, however, financial planners and some financial advisors with more and more expertise in succession planning who can be a valuable resource to a business owner. Such an advisor can not only bring some specialized expertise to the table, but many times can help reduce the legal expenses associated with business succession planning.

CHAPTER 30

When Family *Is* the Business Succession Plan

What's the difference between a lawyer and an onion?

Jamie Hargrove

You cry when you cut up an onion.

As I mentioned in Chapter 29, business succession planning is an important consideration whether family members are involved or not. Owning and operating a business comes with a variety of challenges in the best of circumstances. When that business becomes a family affair involving children, siblings and others across several generations, it becomes even more complex. When dealing with loved ones both involved in the business and not involved, you can quickly have issues about "fairness" and "equality." What is fair and equal in the context of a family business and estate planning when dealing with two very different groups of family members?

There is no universal answer to that question. Every family situation and business is unique. When one or more family members become involved in your business, you often face a host of planning issues and challenges. Most of those issues come from conflicting perspectives. Best business practices may call for one course of action, while family dynamics call for another. I'm going to discuss this in terms of children working in a family business, but the suggestions and information are applicable regardless of whether it's a child, sibling or another family member.

Scenario #1: The undercompensated child

If a child is actively driving the success of the business, that child's ownership stake should be more substantial than if he or she is simply carrying out daily tasks, right? Too often, however, a son or daughter involved in the parents' business is treated less favorably than a non-related "key employee."

If an equity ownership plan is in place to attract and retain non-related key employees, such a plan should also be available to a son or daughter involved in the business. For example, you may offer a 40% ownership interest with a 10-year vesting period to a key employee, but you only offer a son or daughter in a similar position a 10% stake, simply for being related to you. You may think he or she will ultimately get a bigger share via inheritance.

This could be unfair to your child and other employees and could ultimately wreak havoc in the work environment.

Scenario #2: The overcompensated child

Another situation you want to avoid when it comes to estate planning and your family business is one in which a child working in the business is treated in such a fashion that your other children lose out.

I have seen many cases in my career where one son or daughter in a family business receives (via gift or inheritance) virtually all equity/ownership interest in the business. While there are certainly situations where this is reasonable, it most often is unfair to the other children. It might make sense if the business had no value when the son or daughter became involved, and that one child single-handedly breathed life into an otherwise dead company. But in cases where it was older generations who established a thriving company, leaving it in full to a child who did not truly earn it is likely to cause major conflict among the remaining siblings. The portion of a family business that is not directly tied to the contributions made by the family member/ key employee should become a part of the parent's estate, to be divided among all the children. That doesn't mean that the family member involved in the company can't still succeed to 100% of the business. That can be accomplished by giving the key family member the ability to take the company as a part of his or her share of the inheritance, while other siblings take other assets of a comparable value. Alternatively, the key family member could have a right to purchase the business from the estate, with the estate financing the buy-out.

Stock as an employee benefit vs. stock as inheritance

To attract and retain key talent in a family business, owners many times must be prepared to offer both third parties and working family members an ownership stake in the company. This may be appropriate while the owner is still living, or as a part of a well-communicated succession plan triggered at the owner's death or disability. The succession plan should include plans for any portion of the family business that will be sold or liquidated pursuant to the owner's Last Will and Testament and/ or trust.

If you hope to leave the company to a child who is working in the family business while being fair to other children, consider giving the working child a portion of stock equal in value to their contribution. (Consider what it might take to bring in an outside person to do your child's job, and treat the child at least as well as you would that third party.) The difference between the value of that child's contribution and the total value of the company would become a family asset to be divided among all children in your estate, including the child working in the business. If you want the child working in the business to eventually obtain full ownership of it upon your death, there are several options. Here are four:

1. **Buy-Sell Agreement:** Enter into a non-insurance buy-sell agreement that grants the family member a right to purchase the remaining stock at the time of the owner's disability or death. The buy-sell can provide for financing the purchase over a number of years.

2. **Insurance-backed Buy-Sell Agreement (cross purchase):** The family member can secure life insurance on the owner and use the cash proceeds to purchase the stock at the owner's death.

3. **Insurance-backed Buy-Sell Agreement (stock redemption):** If the child already has some company stock, an alternative is for the company to purchase the life insurance policy on the owner. At the owner's death, the business can make the purchase, called a stock redemption. Effectively, the owner's stock vanishes, leaving sole ownership with the employed

child. So for example, assume that a daughter owned 20 shares and dad owned 80 shares at the time of his death. If the company owns the insurance policy and redeems dad's stock out of his estate, the daughter's 20 shares become the only outstanding shares issued and represent 100% of the ownership of the company.

4. **Direct Disposition of Stock Under Last Will and Testament:**

   a. <u>Assets to balance stock gift:</u> Dad can allocate the stock to his daughter at his death via his Last Will and Testament or trust and allocate other assets in his estate to his other children to equalize the bequests.

   b. <u>No other assets to balance stock gift:</u> If there are no other assets to allocate to the other children that are sufficient to equalize the gift of stock to the employed daughter, the estate (will or trust) can give to the daughter the option to purchase the stock out of the estate or trust. If necessary, the estate or trust can allow for the stock to be paid for, in part or in total, with a promissory note that can then be assigned to the other children.

EXAMPLE:

One daughter works in the business. Her parent/owner believes the value of her contribution is equal to one-third of the company's total value, which is $1.5 million. Other assets in the estate are valued at $3.5 million. The daughter has two siblings, neither of whom work in the business. Here's how an equal division of inheritance might work:

- Daughter already owns one-third of company, which is not part of her inheritance.

- Daughter receives remaining two-thirds of company as her portion of her parent's total estate, valued at $1 million. Siblings each receive $1 million from remaining estate to offset the first daughter's receipt of two-thirds of the business. The remaining $1.5 million ($3.5 million less the two, $1 million equalizing bequests) is divided equally among all three of the children.

- The result is as follows:
    - Daughter owns 100% of company and has additional $500,000;

    - The other two siblings have $1.5 million each. There is an equal inheritance among the three.

In a second scenario, there are not sufficient assets to equalize the inheritance among all the children. In this case, I recommend that the "family" portion of the business shares pass to the estate. This will give all the children the ability to share the value of the family's portion of the company. The child working in the business, however, could then buy the company from the siblings, with the resulting note passing to the siblings to be paid over time, pursuant to the terms of a buy-sell agreement. Such a buy-out might be based on a formula calculation for the fair market value of the business.

In all of these scenarios, I recommend evaluating the use of life insurance to provide the funding for at least a portion of the buy-out. The insurance would be on the life of the father in the above examples, with the policy being owned by the business, the daughter in the business or the father (or his insurance trust). It would be used to provide additional cash and equalize distributions to the other children.

Evaluating a child's contribution to your business

When evaluating a child's contribution to your business, there are numerous factors to consider. First, how significant is the parent/owner's capital and other financial support? If I, as a parent, offered the same level of financial backing to my other children, could they have financial opportunities that might rival whatever my son or daughter has done with my support for them in the family business?

Next, consider whether your working son or daughter has dramatically added to or expanded the family business. Did he or she simply accomplish what any family member could have done if given the same opportunity?

Rather than giving your child company stock, think about selling it to them. If you can predict that a business is going to grow as a direct result of your son or daughter's efforts, an early buy-in by your child can be important not only from a fairness standpoint, but also from a tax angle.

As an example, say a son comes into a business that is worth $1 million. Twenty years later, if the son has grown the business value to $20 million, it would be unfair to divide a $25 million estate among four children, three of whom did not make significant contributions to the business. If a deal is struck so that the parent and child are effectively partners in the future of the business, then "unfairness" issues can be better addressed.

Other issues of ownership and asset allocation

Problems may result from minority ownership interests in a family business. As a general rule, I don't suggest that family members who do not actually work in a business have an ownership stake. In virtually every situation I have observed, it has led to discord. Questions posed by the "silent" partner about salary, benefits or management decisions can cause problems for the other family members who are running the show.

This chapter is about family members in a family business succeeding to the business upon the death of the primary owner. While I have not talked about that succession happening via a trust, the use of one or more trusts should be considered to protect the business interest from spousal rights, creditor's claims and potential estate and inheritance tax in younger generations. So for example, if a child plans to invest in or purchase an ownership stake in the family business, consider setting up a trust and making the purchase by the trust instead of directly by the child. See Chapter 19 for more discussion of the use and benefit of a trust to start or grow a business.

You will also want to give adequate consideration to the role of your non-related key employees and how retaining them may impact your plans to pass on the business at your death. Many key management employees may not be interested in working for a business unless they are offered the chance to buy out the business upon the death of the founder. It's important to work with your key employee to create a well-thought-out, written succession plan to address such a situation. This will help the key employee trust that he or she "has a future" at the company once the founder has passed away. You must be proactive on this issue, or your key employee(s) may be out the door before you realize there's a problem.

Finally, as noted earlier, the goal in family business succession planning often is to arrange for other non-business assets to offset the inheritance of the child working in the business. One way to help equalize inheritance among siblings is to set aside and manage any non-essential business assets (investment portfolios, cash accounts, etc.) independently. This reduces the value of the business and increases the value of non-company assets. You could also separate the business' real estate from the operating company and choose to leave those real estate holdings to non-involved family members. Ownership of the operating company could then be left to just the son or daughter directly involved in the business. A final option is to purchase life insurance on the owner and/or owner's spouse to create additional wealth that is separate from the business. Any of these scenarios would help equalize inheritance among the business owner's other children.

End of Lawyers? No, lawyers are safe here. Family business succession plans and family dynamics both inside and outside a business are complex issues that involve lots of moving parts. A lawyer can address all the issues that will arise in family businesses, particularly those with children in line to eventually succeed to the business.

CHAPTER 31

Saving the Family Farm

What's the difference between
a dead dog in the road
and a dead lawyer in the road?

Jamie Hargrove

There are skid marks in front of the dog.

I've spent some time discussing general business succession planning and estate planning related to the family business, but what if the business in question is a family farm?

One of the reasons U.S. Congress has significantly increased the estate tax exemption is to save the family farm. A very low exemption (historically in the 1980s and 1990s, only $600,000) was a reason why some farms had to be sold after the owner's death in order to pay taxes.

While I support the larger estate tax exemption and agree it is needed to benefit family farm owners, in the 30-plus years of my practice, I never worked with a client who had to sell the family farm to pay estate taxes. No doubt that it happened to some people, but in my opinion, it was not as prevalent as politicians declared. Those politicians simply had an agenda to promote, and the family farm was certainly a wise ally.

So with the estate tax threat to the family farm now mitigated, is there still a need to discuss "saving the family farm?" The answer is yes.

A family farm is no different from any other business. There **_must_** be a business succession plan related to the farm and farming operations. Too often, a farmer makes optimistic assumptions about how his family will work together to continue farm operations once he is gone.

While a family farm needs a business succession plan like any other business, farming is not like any other business. Because a farm is so much a part of family life, what might work as a business succession plan for a manufacturing or a services company is not going to fly with a family farm.

Family farms can often be tied into the family patriarch's residence, as well as his children's. How many times have you seen a family living in a widget factory or the professional building where the family service business, such as an insurance agency or physician's practice, operates? I'm betting not many. But, of course, families often live and work on their farms.

While there are certainly some businesses that are difficult to separate from their physical locations, none are more so than a farming operation. So then, the argument arises about whether a farming operation is more like a simple real estate investment than a widget company or service business. Is owning a farm and farming operation anything like owning commercial real estate? No. Is it like owning and managing apartments and other residential real estate? Not much in common there, either.

A farming operation has its own unique challenges, including family dynamics. For example, what needs to be factored into the farm's planning relative to in-laws? Should the sons- or daughters-in-law have any input on its succession plan? Well, if your plan is going to involve your kids, then yes, you'd better, at least in part, involve their spouses. In most business succession plans, it is very rare for a family member's spouse to ultimately succeed to operation of the business. This is an area, however, where family farms are different — much different. Farming is not only a business; it's a lifestyle. Because it's a lifestyle, it has a greater impact on the family than any other business or occupation. If there is not total buy-in from the spouse of the future farmer or future manager of the farm, then your farm succession plan is going to have problems. Too often, the succession plan conceived by the head of the farming family is never discussed, let alone carried out. The interests of the children and their spouses in continuing the farm's operations are often not addressed in a direct enough fashion for any cohesive plan to be developed.

The process of planning

Business succession planning or farm succession planning is often viewed as something that needs to evolve around a business document. That is absolutely not the case. The business document needs to evolve around the plan, not vice versa.

While you might need a lawyer, financial planner, accountant or other professional to facilitate meetings and discussions to determine the targeted farm succession plan, it does not need to start with a document or with a bunch of numbers. Documents, numbers and analyses can all fall in place after the family determines how, when and in what manner the succession of the farm will be handled.

For a very basic roadmap of the initial workings of a farm succession plan, consider these steps:

- **<u>Step 1:</u>** Start with a meeting that involves the entire family. Invite spouses and significant others. I suggest having someone facilitate the meeting. This may be your accountant, lawyer or financial advisor.

    Make it clear that this meeting is not a decision-making meeting; it is simply a chance for everyone in the family to offer his or her thoughts about the long-term future of the farm and its operations. Mom and Dad can share their thoughts, expectations and view of the future, or simply remain silent and let the other family members have their say.

    The goal for this meeting is to gather information and identify any conflicting views or perceptions, encourage the in-laws to comment and participate, as they may be the ones who will be the most direct and honest.

    Have a note taker who is not a family member. This can be the facilitator or another neutral person. It is important to capture relevant comments and who said them, so they can be used at the next meeting.

- **Step 2:** Within a few weeks of the first meeting, set up a second meeting with children but without their spouses or significant others. Just like the first meeting, make it clear that this is not a decision-making meeting, but a chance for the family to voice their thoughts and comments free from any spousal interaction. If there is a concern about a spouse, people should be open to discuss it, but be careful not to create disharmony among your children.

- **Step 3:** The facilitator should then meet with the current controlling owners (Mom and Dad) to begin working on a game plan. Keep in mind that the plan may involve setting up an outside entity to better facilitate the succession plan. The below example will give you an idea of actions to take, such as surveying separate tracts of property, creating a separate farming operation with a lease or leases of the real estate in the farming operation, etc.

EXAMPLE:

Mom and Dad are in their early 80s and in very good health. Dad farms six days a week. Mom and Dad have three children, two sons and a daughter. Son #1 is active in the farming operation. Son #2 and Daughter are not active in the farm, and do not live close by.

Mom and Dad want Son #1 to take over the farm upon Dad's death or disability. This is even if Mom survives Dad. Mom is not active in the farming operations and does not want the responsibility for any aspect of it.

Mom and Dad want Son #1 to operate the farm but also want to leave the farm in equal shares to all three of their children.

Plan 1: A surveyor works with the family and the three kids to divide up the farm into three separate tracts, with each tract designated to go to a particular child. At the same time, a family limited liability company (LLC) is established to operate the farm. All of the livestock and equipment is transferred into the farming LLC. The farming LLC is left exclusively to Son #1. Other (non-farming) assets in the estate are left to Son #2 and Daughter as an offset to the farming operation passing to Son #1.

*(**NOTE:** By moving the farming operations into a separate LLC with only the cattle and equipment, the total value of the farming operations is minimized. In other words, we pull the real estate out and treat it separately.)*

Dad's Last Will and Testament (or living trust) is redrafted to provide for the above as well as for separate tracts of the farm to pass to each of the three kids. This is based on their input and interest in the particular tracts.

Perhaps the farm is not divisible into three tracts, but only into two tracts. You could leave the larger tract to Son #2 and Daughter and the smaller tract to Son #1. Maybe there is a buy/sell arrangement under which Son #1 pays Son #2 and Daughter some amount of money over a certain time period to effectively buy out part of the larger tract that Daughter and Son #2 receive.

*(**NOTE:** The goal is to try to carve out as much as you can into equal, separate shares. Separate shares are always a better option than single shares left to multiple family members. The goal is to leave the farm in such a way that if it still makes sense to operate the entire farm as a single entity and everyone gets*

along, you have a structure that will allow for that to happen. If, on the other hand, there is family discord, then there is already a built-in way to unplug and change the structure of the farming operation.)

Dad enters into leases between himself and the farming LLC. The leases can have renewal options, so Son #1 is assured he will have a certain number of years he can continue farming and know that the other tracts are under a set lease agreement for a certain number of years as well. If this is Son #1's only source of income and the only life he has ever known, those lease terms may be set to allow the Son #1 to continue to lease through a certain retirement date/age. The leases can then terminate and allow the other two kids to either re-lease the property or sell the property based on their interests.

Plan 2: If the property is not divisible for any reason, still establish a separate farm operating LLC, and possibly put the farm property in a separate LLC. The farm LLC can have 1% voting interest and 99% non-voting interest. The 1% interest can pass to Son #1, with the 99% passing equally to all three kids.

As with Plan 1, lease agreements should be in place and possibly require a majority vote of all LLC members, in order to be able to amend or otherwise revise the lease terms. Having the lease terms well-defined while Dad is still around leaves time for the kids to contest his decisions and revise them.

*(**NOTE:** The goal here is to ensure that non-farmers who may inherit farmland, but will not directly benefit from its operations, will gain some economic benefit as a result of the lease income. By using voting and non-voting interests in the LLC, Dad no longer has to give Son #1 a 51% interest in an entity in order to*

give the son control. The control piece becomes a very small part of the equity, so that the equity can be more fairly distributed.)

I could go on with another dozen different illustrations and alternatives, but the above should give you an idea of some of the considerations with business planning and the family farm.

Another consideration is life insurance. Unfortunately, farmers do not tend to be big advocates of life insurance. Had Mom and Dad secured life insurance many years ago when it was affordable, they could potentially have had two sets of primary assets rather than just one. The second set would be the cash proceeds from the life insurance, which could be utilized to provide some or all of the inheritance to the non-farming children. In that case, a lot of the complications of Plans 1 and 2 above could be eliminated or minimized.

While an 80-year-old couple will find securing life insurance a challenge, younger farmers should give serious consideration to including permanent life insurance in their planning. There really is no better example of a need for life insurance than with the family farm, where the goal is to continue the farm into the next generation.

End of Lawyers? Not in this case. With all of the unique problems and challenges that face family farmers, it is important for them to seek trained professionals to help with both business succession and estate planning. An attorney experienced in dealing with farmers is a must. Many business lawyers are great at handling widget companies, but maybe not so great when it comes to the family farm.

CHAPTER 32

Employee Stock Incentive Plan: Stock vs. Phantom Stock

*Why did God make snakes
just before lawyers?*

Jamie Hargrove

To practice.

When discussing succession planning, often the transfer of company stock during the owner's life is a consideration. Awarding stock ownership is one way to communicate your commitment to a key employee or reward a family member employed by the company.

If the company has one class of stock, then all stockholders have voting power. This is most often "what comes out of the box" when a corporation is first established, unless the owners have directed their business attorney otherwise. This means that there will be a limitation on the amount of equity that can be transferred to a key employee or family members without giving up control, usually less than 50%. The owner will need to keep slightly more than 50% of the company stock to maintain control.

A company can always recapitalize its corporate stock and create two classes, most often a voting common stock class and a non-voting common stock class. Even S corporations[9] that are limited to only one class of stock may have two classes if they are identical except for voting rights. One class of stock can have voting power while the other class has no voting power.

Other types of entities, such as limited liability companies, can also be created with voting units and non-voting membership units. Both voting and non-voting units in an LLC and stock in a corporation can be structured so that the voting interests are a small percentage of the overall equity of the company. The non-voting interests can constitute the majority of the equity.

For example, a commonly used business capitalization allows 95% of the capital in the company to be in the form of non-voting stock or non-voting membership interests, with 5% of the equity in the company in voting stock or voting membership

---

9 An S corporation is a business entity organized as a corporation but with a special tax election to be treated as a type of pass-through entity for income tax purposes. So a corporation, for tax purposes, will either be a C corporation (no tax election made) or an S corporation (tax election made). The election only impacts the income tax treatment of the entity. It has no impact on the legal liability or organizational structure of the entity.

interests. This will allow a business owner to transfer up to 95% of the company's equity to key employees, family members or trusts for estate planning without giving up any of the voting control. Consequently, 100% of the vote is maintained, while potentially only 5% of the equity is retained.

As I discussed in the prior chapters, business interests transferred to children should be transferred to them in trust, not outright. This is the case even when the business interests being transferred are non-voting.

While there are tremendous benefits from putting stock in the hands of key employees (either family members or non-family members), there are also some disadvantages. Once stock is issued to an individual, he becomes a legal shareholder with all of the rights that a particular state's statutes may give such shareholder. Sometimes, those rights can be limited, but too often they cannot. In a few states, for example, once stock is granted to an individual, an agreement that allows the stock to be bought back at nominal value if the employee leaves the company (or upon some other triggering event) may be unenforceable. Part of what state statutes attempt to do is to protect minority shareholders. Again, those protections vary from state to state.

If stock is to be granted to an employee, it should be accompanied with a shareholder agreement that outlines all of the rights and buy-back options, etc. An experienced attorney familiar with your state's statutes will need to advise you as to what you can and cannot include in such an agreement, as well as what areas may be problematic with such stock ownership.

One right that shareholders — even minority shareholders — have is the right to access the books and records of the company. In most states, this is a right that cannot be limited or restricted by contract.

Just as an aside, when you create the agreement regarding the issuance of your business interests to a key employee or family member, make sure to ask your attorney to include non-competition language. The issuance of stock is a good time to bind the key employee to non-compete provisions. For such non-compete provisions to be enforceable in most states, certain considerations must be given. Consideration cannot be the threat of firing or an agreement to continue employment.

One solution to the problems that can be associated with a non-compete agreement might be to implement a phantom stock plan. In my practice, I call a phantom stock plan an Employee Stock Incentive Plan (ESIP). I do not use a reference to phantom stock since that seems to belittle the value of the plan in the eyes of some employees.

Some of the characteristics of an ESIP are:

- Units can be used to reward key employees;

- Units usually have value only if the company prospers;

- Units can be granted without triggering income tax consequences to either the company or the employee;

- ESIPs can give key employees some of the same benefits of stock ownership without the problems created by minority stock ownership.

An ESIP is effectively an employee contract or agreement. It is not an actual grant of stock. If you think about it, what an employee really wants is the opportunity to participate in the profits of the company if it is successful, or participate in the proceeds if the company is ever sold.

An ESIP can be structured so that if the employee is given a 10% ESIP stock plan, the following would apply:

- The employee will receive a bonus each year equal to 10% of the profits distributed by the company. As an example, if the company distributes a dividend of $100,000, the key employee will receive $10,000 as a bonus.

- If the business is sold, pursuant to the ESIP, the key employee would receive 10% of the proceeds from the sale. This, too, will be effectively treated as a bonus to the key employee.

- Many times, even with an ESIP, the key employee is also allowed to enter into a separate employment agreement — similar to a buy/sell agreement — that may allow him or her to buy into the company stock at the owner's death.

The tax implications of the ESIP favor the company. For example, when the owner sells the company, he will be able to treat the funds that pass to the key employee under the ESIP as deductible compensation and take a tax deduction on its final return. The employee, on the other hand, does not have as favorable treatment, since the employee will receive such benefits as ordinary income with no opportunity for categorizing them as capital gains.

If, instead, the employee had owned stock in the company or membership interests in an LLC for longer than a year and was vested in those interests, the employee would receive capital gains treatment. I have found, however, that most key employees are simply happy to be participating in the future success of the company, and the tax issues are not the focus when the plan is set up.

End of Lawyers? No. This area involves multiple legal issues. Many of those may not simply be statutory but can be a matter of law resulting from court case rulings. An attorney specializing in business law should always be consulted when setting up any type of stock or ESIP plan.

TAX DEFERRED ACCOUNTS/
LIFE INSURANCE

CHAPTER 33

IRAs and 401(k)s: Stretching the Tax Benefits

What's the difference between lawyers and buzzards?

Jamie Hargrove

Lawyers have removable wing tips.

,

Some of the greatest wealth-building vehicles include IRAs, 401(k)s and similar plans. With income tax rates on the rise, the ability to accumulate and grow assets tax-deferred is a valuable option. A key estate planning opportunity is to determine how best to "stretch," and thus maximize, the value and benefits of these tax-deferred accounts.

My goal in many cases is simply to defer the realization of the beneficiary's income from the account as long as possible. With an IRA, it may be as simple as designating your spouse as the beneficiary, with your adult children as the secondary beneficiaries. A spouse is entitled to a 100% rollover. [10] This allows a spouse to continue to defer recognizing income from the IRA until he or she reaches age 70 ½, at which point his or her remaining life expectancy will determine the required minimum distributions (RMDs). If there is no surviving spouse, the adult children will have the opportunity to withdraw from the account over their life expectancy, based on certain IRS tables.[11]

It is this ability to take required minimum distributions over the beneficiary's lifetime that creates a "stretch" opportunity. Simply put, we often want to stretch out the benefits so we can, in the meantime, defer more taxes. The longer the stretch, the longer the deferral. Further, the longer the stretch, the longer the asset-protection aspects of the IRA continue. Generally, assets in an IRA are protected from the claims of creditors of the person setting up and contributing to the account, as well as from the claims of a beneficiary's creditors. So, the longer you can stretch

---

10 The general rule for a deceased person's account is that if the account is left to a spouse, the spouse may elect to "roll over" the balance into another account in the survivor's name. At that point, the account is subject to the same rules as if it had always been the account of the surviving spouse. This means that if the surviving spouse has not attained the age of 70 ½, the surviving spouse will not be required to take any required minimum distributions (RMDs), until reaching age 70 ½.

11 Unlike a spouse, children (along with any other non-spouse beneficiary) are not allowed to roll over the account into an account in their own name. Instead, the non-spouse beneficiary has only one deferral option, which is to receive the funds from his or her share of the account over his or her lifetime based on RMDs calculated on the non-spouse beneficiary's age.

the payout and keep more in the IRA, the longer you keep assets protected.

In situations where the children are minors, spendthrifts, or for other reasons you want to protect or control their IRA distributions, consider creating an IRA trust. An IRA trust is designed specifically to serve as a beneficiary of an IRA or other qualified plan account. It will allow the account distributions to "stretch" over the life expectancy of the beneficiary of such trust.[12]

Individuals who have grandchildren may set up IRA trusts for them so as to use the grandchildren's young age as the determining factor for the RMDs. If you want to maximize the "stretch" (i.e., deferral), then you'll want to name grandchildren as beneficiaries, not your children. Again, it is the grandchild's age that becomes the measuring life for the purposes of calculating the RMD each year.[13] Without an IRA trust, naming a young child or a grandchild as a beneficiary may give too much control and access to the IRA account too soon. If you name a grandchild as a direct beneficiary of your IRA, he or she can take advantage of the "stretch" aspect of an IRA, and no trust is required for him or her to do so. The problem, of course, is that there is also nothing that will keep the grandchild from pulling out the entire IRA balance once he reaches age 18. The IRA trust can protect against this situation.

In my practice, I generally separate an IRA trust into separate trusts for each grandchild (or child, if that is the case). This allows for maximization of the stretch when there

---

12 While an account left directly to a beneficiary can be "stretched" for income tax purposes, without a trust, the beneficiary can withdraw as much as he or she chooses and spend the funds in any manner the beneficiary desires. If, on the other hand, the funds pass to an IRA/pension trust, the terms of the trust will dictate what happens to the funds. They can be controlled by the trustee and protected from spousal and creditor rights.

13 Not only does the IRA/Pension Trust allow for stretching the account for tax purposes, it allows the trustee of the IRA/Pension Trust to control when and how the distributions beyond the RMDs are received by the trust and, ultimately, by the beneficiary of the IRA/Pension Trust.

are multiple children and grandchildren at varying ages. For example, if you combine an adult son and his two minor children in an IRA trust, the measuring life for the RMDs becomes the oldest beneficiary, which in that example would be the child. The ages of the minor grandchildren, unfortunately, do not impact the calculation of the RMDs. The stretch or deferral of the IRA is minimized as a result of combining younger and older beneficiaries in one trust. If each beneficiary has a separate trust, each beneficiary's life expectancy is the determining factor for the RMDs' calculation in his or her particular trust.

End of Lawyers? Probably. Financial advisors and planners have often been ahead of lawyers in understanding the ins and outs of retirement planning. If anything, online technology may actually help lawyers overcome some of their knowledge shortfalls in the IRA and qualified plan world. If lawyers adopt online programs and use them to help deliver efficient advice, they may keep their jobs in this area.

CHAPTER 34

Life Insurance: Term vs. Permanent and Other Considerations

What's the definition of a lawyer?

Jamie Hargrove

A mouth with a life support system.

People often ask me if, as an estate planning attorney, I sell life insurance. Yes and no. No, I do not technically sell life insurance, receive any commission, compensation or other remuneration when a client buys such insurance. But I do sell the concept and point out the need for life insurance because it is a very important tool when it comes to families and estate planning.

I have never met with a family after a death where anyone complained about having too much insurance on the life of the deceased person. On the other hand, I cannot count the number of situations I have encountered when too little life insurance was in place, which created significant challenges for either the surviving spouse, other family members or a family business.

The big question is whether to buy term insurance or permanent insurance. Certainly, there are situations where term life insurance is all a family may need. For example, a husband and wife have several children; the husband makes a nice living and the wife stays home with the kids. Should something happen to her husband, the wife would not want to disrupt her family by taking one or more jobs to replace her deceased husband's lost income. Having some term insurance in place on the husband that would replace his income while the children are still at home is a good solution. For young couples, the cost of this type of insurance is very inexpensive. If the stay-at-home wife wants to go back to work, no problem. What the life insurance will do is give the wife options. Options are good. Without life insurance, options are limited.

Many times, I advise my clients to consider investing in permanent insurance (e.g., universal life, whole life or no lapse guarantee) instead of term insurance. As time goes by, a stay-at-home mom may become less and less marketable in the workforce. Depending on how old she is at the time the children finally leave the nest, it may be challenging for her to find employment that would replace the income lost at her husband's death. Too often, by that time the term insurance has expired or is too expensive to continue. The stay-at-home mom then finds herself in a position where her standard of living may significantly decrease.

Statistics show that less than 2% of the death benefits paid in the United States are paid out of a term policy. That may be why such policies are so cheap. They basically insure you when there is little risk that you are going to die. When you get older and really need the insurance, it then becomes cost-prohibitive to maintain. Consequently, the insurance gets dropped, and you have no insurance in place to protect your family when you die.

There are financial planners who will argue you should "buy term and invest the difference." I have been in practice for over 30 years, and I have never seen that strategy work. On paper, it seems to make a lot of sense. It certainly made a lot of sense when interest rates and returns were a lot higher than they are today. But it only works if, in fact, you do invest the difference. Unfortunately, I have never seen the "difference" invested in something that provides a meaningful return.

The next question about life insurance you need to consider is how much coverage to buy. I use a very simple formula to get me in the ballpark of how much insurance a person needs. The formula is as follows:

Annual cash flow needed to replace lost cash flow / 0.05 – current investable assets

So let's assume that your target for income replacement is $100,000. If you divide $100,000 by 0.05, you get $2 million. If you then have $400,000 in marketable securities and 401(k) account funds, you subtract the $400,000 from the $2 million, which gets you to $1.6 million in needed insurance benefits.

Let's take another look at those numbers. Assume you are the stay-at-home parent who needs to replace $100,000 of income when your spouse dies. If you invest your $1.6 million in insurance proceeds along with your $400,000 in other investments, you'll have $2 million under investment. With a 5% annual withdrawal right, you will receive $100,000 a year. The goal would be to spend 5% of your principal base each year. Your total return on such invested assets (counting principal growth, interest and dividends) should be greater than 5%. By taking 5%, you should be able to continue to grow your investment pool so that each year your 5% is taken from a little bit larger investment base, which means your payment will be a little larger.

When you look at insurance from the perspective of creating an investment base from which you withdraw a percentage of the value each year, it makes the amount of insurance you need go up significantly. If you approach it any other way, the surviving spouse may run out of money, and will probably do so at a point when he or she is least able to secure viable employment.

Life insurance and trusts

An irrevocable life insurance trust has been a staple in the estate planning world for a long time. Because of the significant increase in the estate tax exemption to well over $5 million, the necessity of an irrevocable life insurance trust is no longer as significant as it once was. If an insurance trust is not utilized, the insurance should still be directed to a trust for the benefit of a spouse, children and/or other family members as appropriate. It can go to a living trust, if one already exists. If no other trusts have been set up for this purpose, you may want to consider an irrevocable life insurance trust.

For example, a lot of my clients prefer to have their life insurance left to a spouse in an irrevocable life insurance trust to protect the proceeds from claims of a future spouse or creditors. Having the proceeds from the life insurance in an irrevocable life insurance trust can grant the surviving spouse broad rights, access and even control as trustee, but still allow the assets to be free from any claims or marital rights that a second marriage of the surviving spouse might impose.

In my law practice, if a client needs an insurance trust, I often combine it with family protection trust planning, discussed in Chapter 9. In this situation, the irrevocable life insurance trust becomes not only the trust that holds the life insurance proceeds, but also a silo that all other trusts and Last Wills and Testaments "pour into" when a husband or wife dies. The trust then provides lifetime protection trusts for children and other descendants. If there are multiple children, the trust may break into separate and distinct trusts with each child having his or her own trust.

As a general rule, a husband's insurance and a wife's insurance should not be placed in the same trust. This means that the husband's insurance needs to go into a trust that benefits the wife, but such trust should not own policies under which the wife is the insured. Those policies will need to have separate trusts. If you have multiple insurance trusts, you generally would have one serve as the family protection trust. At the death of the surviving spouse, have the second insurance trust "pour over" into the family protection trust, along with all other trusts in the estates.

End of Lawyers? Maybe. While you can purchase life insurance from many reputable sources, it is smart to look at such insurance in the context of overall family and estate planning. While some lawyers are well-informed and educated about the various life insurance products available, most life insurance is sold by financial planners and advisors who are better equipped to offer advice not only about the insurance, but also on broader estate planning issues that insurance can impact.

CHAPTER 35

529 Education Savings Plans

Why are lawyers like nuclear weapons?

When they land,
they prevent anything from functioning
for the next hundred years.

Establishing a 529 plan[14] has become a very popular option for children, grandchildren and other close family relations who may need to pay for college education.

U.S. Congress created 529 plans in 1996. One of the reasons they are so popular is because they have been around long enough for financial advisors to fully understand their ins and outs. They have also been the focus of a pretty significant marketing effort. As with many other tax benefits, there are numerous limitations on who can take advantage of a 529 plan, as well as complicated phase-out rules. With a 529 plan, anyone can set up the plan at any time, regardless of income or wealth. The limitations generally relate to how much can be contributed into such tax-advantaged accounts.

A 529 plan can be set up with virtually any financial institution, including most insurance companies. While contributions to a 529 plan are not deductible for federal income tax purposes, the earnings on the account are not taxable. This means that the longer the account exists, the greater the benefit. If you have a 17-year-old who is going to go to college this fall, the 529 plan may not be that beneficial, unless you intend to put money in today that will be used in later years of college or graduate school. To put the funds in now and immediately pull them out in a few months, however, will give you little or no real benefit.

While there is no federal income tax deduction for contributions into a 529 plan, some states do allow a deduction for state income tax purposes. Make sure your tax preparer is aware of any contributions you made to a 529 plan for a given tax year.

---

14 A 529 plan is a tax-advantaged savings plan designed to encourage saving for future college costs. 529 plans, legally known as "qualified tuition plans," are sponsored by states, state agencies or educational institutions and are authorized by Section 529 of the Internal Revenue Code.

Jamie Hargrove

To get the maximum benefit, you need to begin sooner than later with these accounts. If you have a new child or grandchild, setting funds aside now can provide up to 18 years (maybe longer) of tax-free earnings on your contributions.

The amount that can be contributed into a 529 account cannot exceed the amount necessary to provide for the qualified education expenses of the beneficiary. The IRS does not give a precise maximum contribution figure for each 529 plan. Many companies offering 529 plans have software that will help you calculate the amount you can reasonably set aside in each 529 account. For example, when I calculated the amount that I can contribute into my 15-year-old daughter's new 529 account, it came out to $292,000. This is based on her going to a particular liberal arts college in Kentucky. The higher-end software will give you calculations that are based on the fees of a particular college or university. Because there is no set rule by the IRS, and because the money ultimately has to be used for educational expenses, there appears to be little IRS policing of amounts going into the 529 plans.

A contribution into a 529 plan is treated as a "gift" for gift tax purposes. The annual exclusion limitation ($14,000/year) relates only to gift and estate tax planning and has nothing to do with the actual limit on how much can be contributed to a 529 plan. With the estate tax exemption now well over $5 million per individual (over $10 million for a married couple), the gift tax annual limitation is meaningless for most people.

But while I'm on the subject of the annual exclusion limitation for gift and estate tax purposes, let me mention that for high-net-worth individuals, you are able to front-load a 529 plan with the current year's gifting amounts plus four future years. That equates to five years of annual exclusion amounts, which would be $70,000 (5 x $14,000) for each individual for whom an account is established.

If you are a high-net-worth individual for whom these annual exclusions are an important part of your overall estate and gift tax planning, you should at least consider these limitations. However, if you exceed the $14,000/year per beneficiary gift tax exclusion ($70,000 if you front-load) it will simply utilize some of your estate and gift tax exemption (again, over $5 million currently) but will not trigger a gift tax liability, assuming you still have some of your $5 million-plus estate and gift tax exemption.

Many states will allow up to or, in some cases, in excess of $400,000 to be contributed to a 529 plan. This may need some oversight for high-net-worth individuals with estates over $5 million (or $10 million joint) for gift and estate tax purposes. Otherwise, there is really no limitation. To the extent large contributions (anything over $14,000 per beneficiary per year) will trigger the need for a gift tax return, there will not be any gift taxes due, assuming there is a sufficient amount of a person's $5 million exemption available (i.e., has not exhausted his/her exemption with prior taxable gifts). Additionally, for people with estates that are well under $5 million ($10 million joint), there should be no gift or estate tax consequences.

When it comes to limitations on how much a state may allow, they generally are not required to take into account contributions made to plans in other states. Consequently, accounts could be established in multiple states and therefore exceed any given state's limits for an individual beneficiary. Just remember that technically the IRS says you can only contribute an amount "reasonably necessary" to fund the education of the 529 beneficiary.

A 529 plan can be established either as a prepaid tuition plan or as a savings plan. Each state has its own program. These programs, however, are generally marketed through financial institutions. This means that you don't necessarily have to research every state's 529 program. Your financial advisor should be able to make good recommendations. As a general rule, you do not have to live in a particular state to take advantage of that state's 529 plan program, but there may be state income tax issues to consider. Again, your financial advisor can give you his recommendations on what he believes is the best program for your particular situation.

Generally, if the funds are not utilized for education purposes, they can be returned to the custodian of the account. Such return of funds will trigger income taxes on the income earned in the account, plus a 10% penalty. One way to potentially avoid or delay the taxation of such accounts is to change the beneficiary designation to another child or grandchild who may need the funds for his or her educational expenses.

If you have set up plans for your children, you can keep moving the funds down, eventually to your youngest child. If by the time your youngest child gets through college, there still are significant funds remaining, and you have had a grandchild in the meantime, you can make him/her the new beneficiary. The funds are then held for the benefit of the grandchild and will continue to grow tax-free. This is simply a matter of changing the beneficiary designation to the grandchild and thus avoiding any income taxes on the account, as well as any penalties. Remember, it is only if you cancel the plan and take back possession of the account that you trigger income taxes and penalties.

Keep in mind that 529 plans can impact a student's financial aid qualification. A 529 account must be reported on the federal financial aid application (FAFSA) as an asset of the parent. However, whether the funds are sitting in the parents' normal investment account or in the 529 plan, it shouldn't make any difference. What does make a difference is whether the funds are in a 529 plan or in the individual child's name. Parents' assets are not assessed as highly as the student's personal assets for purposes of financial aid calculations. Consequently, having funds in a 529 plan versus having the funds held by the student will usually be better in terms of financial reporting for any federal government programs. Each school can establish its own rules for assessing the financial suitability of a student for its own need-based programs.

The types of educational expenses allowed for a 529 plan are generally tuition, fees, room and board, books and supplies. If the student has secured off-campus housing that is not part of university housing, the amount of housing to be paid out of the 529 plan should not exceed the average cost of housing offered by the university. Any additional rent costs for off-campus living should be paid using another source of funds.

Also, the cost of furnishing an apartment or a dorm room is generally not part of educational expenses. Furniture, television, pots and pans, etc. are not considered educational expenses.

Computers are allowed if the university requires them for attendance. Costs of laptops, iPads, Internet service and software may be allowed if a student receives scholarships. The government now provides for educational enhancements for scholarship students. Such funds for computers and computer-related equipment, however, should not exceed the scholarship funds, unless they are required by the university. If required by the university, they can be paid regardless of whether there are funds remaining as a result of scholarships.

End of Lawyers? The handling of 529 plans generally does not require a lawyer's involvement. While some lawyers certainly are capable of providing advice on 529 plans, many financial advisors are now well equipped to advise you on the details.

SOCIAL SECURITY, GOVERNMENT ASSISTANCE, ETC.

CHAPTER 36

America Gets Older

What's the difference between a lawyer and a catfish?

Jamie Hargrove

One is a slimy, bottom dwelling, scum sucker.

The other is a fish.

As baby boomers are now pouring into the 65-and-over category, America's elder generation is growing at its fastest pace ever. The earliest baby boomers were born between 1946 and 1964. This means that baby boomers started hitting age 65 in 2011. AARP® estimates that over the next 18 years, baby boomers will turn 65 years of age at the rate of approximately 8,000/day[15]. With this increase in today's older population, there is a greater need for specialized services in many areas of estate and retirement planning, including:

- Social Security planning
- Assessment of retirement benefit options
- Planning for government assistance opportunities in dealing with long-term care issues
- Money management
- Disability planning
- Second marriage planning

If you have reached or are approaching retirement age, you should plan to update all aspects of your financial and healthcare planning, and begin to address some of the issues referenced above. If you don't address the important issues now, it may soon be too late. Appointing someone to have authority over your financial and healthcare decisions needs to happen while you still have the competency to do that. When it comes to applying for government assistance (Medicare, Medicaid, disability, Social Security), advance planning is especially crucial. (I will discuss this in more detail in the next chapters.)

Aging is also not the only reason you may become impaired. Your mental competency could change at any age, at any time, with a stroke, car accident or some other unfortunate and unforeseen occurrence, so it's best to be prepared for the

---

15 http://www.aarp.org/personal-growth/transitions/boomers_65/

worst. While an "emergency plan" can be of some help, it is generally not as effective as comprehensive, proactive, long-term planning.

Of course, when we talk about an aging population, we are not only talking about baby boomers, but also their parents or grandparents. Don't assume that Mom, Dad, Grandma or Grandpa have their planning complete. You will most likely be shocked and dismayed to find that, in fact, their planning is woefully out of date, if they have any planning in place at all.

The most responsible and detailed people in the world many times fall short when it comes to planning for their later years. There is probably not an estate planning or elder law attorney practicing today who cannot give you examples of family members coming to them when it's too late, after they have been exposed to the nightmares a lack of planning in this important area can cause. Don't wait — have the tough discussions now with your parents or grandparents. Push gently to see if you can help with the follow-up to make it happen.

Except in rare cases (i.e., no blood relatives are living, competent or trustworthy), if you are an in-law to an elderly relative I suggest you never be the one to push these issues. Ask your spouse or other blood relative to facilitate the process. Only in very few situations have I seen an in-law be effective in that role. The few times were when the in-law offered his or her professional services. For example, you may be a lawyer who is already providing legal services, or you may be an investment advisor providing financial services to the family. In those situations, you already are a trusted advisor, so your advice will likely be viewed as an extension of the other work you do for them. When you do not have those existing connections, however, it is dangerous to be pushy in getting such planning accomplished.

End of Lawyers? Maybe, but probably not. As America gets older, legal and financial issues become more complex. When you combine issues concerning financial decisions, mental competency, government assistance, long-term care and a host of others, a trained elder law or estate planning attorney can be invaluable.

CHAPTER 37

Social Security Retirement Benefits

What do you call a smiling, sober,
courteous person at a
bar association convention?

Jamie Hargrove

The caterer.

Social Security and Medicare are government programs that impact every U.S. citizen who reaches a certain age or experiences another triggering event. Social Security, as most people know, is generally associated with a retirement benefit when we reach retirement age. Social Security also deals with disability and survivors' benefits. Medicare is a separate governmental program that helps pay for inpatient hospital care, short-term nursing home care, doctors' fees, prescriptions and other medical services to people age 65 and older. Medicaid generally covers benefits for long-term care. This chapter will focus solely on Social Security retirement benefits.

When it comes time to calculate or estimate your Social Security retirement benefits as you approach retirement, the number of factors that may impact your calculations and choices can be a bit mind-boggling. For most people, however, it really is pretty simple – defer! While approximately 75% of Social Security recipients begin their benefits at age 62, most probably shouldn't.

There are some basics you will need to understand and a few terms to be defined. Your options for choosing when to begin receiving benefits are generally as follows:

- **Age 62**: Everyone, regardless of their current age, has the option to retire for Social Security purposes at the age of 62.

- **Age 65-67:** Somewhere at or between ages 65 and 67, you are going to reach your "full retirement age." If you look at publications produced by the Department of Social Security, they will all refer to your "full retirement age," which depends on when you were born. If you were born in 1937 or earlier, then your full retirement age is 65. If you were born in 1960 or later, your full retirement age is 67. For those born between 1937 and 1960, refer to the table below.

Year of Birth*	Full Retirement Age
1937 or earlier	65
1938	65 and 2 months
1939	65 and 4 months
1940	65 and 6 months
1941	65 and 8 months
1942	65 and 10 months
1943-1954	66
1955	66 and 2 months
1956	66 and 4 months
1957	66 and 6 months
1958	66 and 8 months
1959	66 and 10 months
1960 and later	67

*If you were born on Jan. 1st of any year, you should refer to the previous year. (If you were born on the 1st of the month, your benefit (and your full retirement age) is determined as if your birthday were in the previous month.)

Source: http://www.socialsecurity.gov/retire2/retirechart.htm#chart

Your Social Security retirement benefits are adjusted for inflation each year. This inflation adjustment not only applies once you start receiving benefits, but also applies to the calculation of your future benefits. The inflation adjustment for 2015, for example, was 1.7%. In 2014, it was 1.5% and in 2013, it was 1.7%. Previous cost-of-living adjustments have ranged from zero in 2010 and 2011 to 14.3% in 1980.

So when do I start?

As mentioned above, about three-fourths of people entitled to receive their Social Security retirement benefits start taking their benefits at age 62. Financial advisors who really understand this area, however, will tell you that most people should probably delay their benefits until their normal retirement age (age 65 – 67), or even age 70.

Some of the reasons you might want to take the benefit early (or defer it) are as follows:

1. **You need the money:** If you simply need the money and you have no alternative sources of income, then you may not have an option. You may have to start your benefits early at age 62.

    Remember, however, if you have other retirement benefits, and depending upon whether you're going to trigger income taxes on your Social Security benefits, you may want to consider using other retirement benefits rather than applying for Social Security at age 62.

2. **Shortened life expectancy:** If you are single and have a shortened life expectancy, you probably will want to start your benefits early. This will depend upon your actual life expectancy, and potentially other factors. The Social Security calculations are designed so that if you live your normal life expectancy, the increased benefits in later years will "make up" for the years that you delayed and didn't take any benefits. If your life expectancy is shortened, then you won't have as many years to catch up on the delayed payments. Consequently, you may want to begin your benefits sooner than later.

    If on the other hand, you have a shortened life expectancy and have a spouse, you may actually be better off deferring until your normal retirement date, as your death between the early retirement date and the normal retirement date can negatively, and potentially substantially, impact your spouse's lifetime benefits. If your spouse has his or her own Social Security retirement benefits that are equal to or greater than yours, then this concern won't be a factor. But when you have a spouse who will eventually share or take over your benefits, then (with a shortened life expectancy) you may still want to delay until your normal retirement age or even until age 70.

If both you and your spouse have a shortened life expectancy, consider taking your benefits sooner (age 62) than later.

3. **Big alternative investment returns:** Even if you don't need to live on your Social Security retirement benefits, and even if you have a normal life expectancy, you may still want to start receiving your benefits at age 62, and invest those at a high rate of return. If your return is high enough, it may be possible for you to come out ahead by the time you reach your normal retirement age (or age 70). Your earnings on the early retirement benefits that were re-invested and accumulated when added to your ongoing benefits from your Social Security retirement may all add up to create a larger benefit for you. This would require, however, a very high return on your invested retirement funds. It may also depend on whether you're paying taxes on such early withdrawal benefits. All of this will factor into the analysis. Some advisors and calculators would point toward the need to secure a 9-10% after-tax growth on the early withdrawal benefits in order to make the numbers work to support the early withdrawal. When you compare the risk of getting a high rate of return or growth to the guarantees provided by the Social Security retirement program, this is not going to be a consideration for very many people.

Keep on working (reduced benefits?):

Retiring for Social Security retirement benefit purposes does not mean you cannot still work. You can earn as much as you want to, once you reach your full retirement age. However, working prior to reaching your full retirement age — and the income you receive from your work — may impact your Social Security benefits if you have elected to take early retirement benefits.

Social Security beneficiaries who are under age 66 can earn as much as $15,720 in 2015. For earnings over $15,720, however, $1 in benefits will be withheld for every $2 earned above the $15,720 limit.

In the year that you reach your full retirement age, the calculation gets more favorable. First off, during the year you reach full retirement age, the deduction drops to only $1 for every $3 earned, not for every $2 earned. Plus, the amount you earn also significantly increases. In 2015, for example, that number is $41,880 rather than only $15,720 if you haven't reached the year of full retirement age. This means that in the year that you reach your full retirement age, you can make $41,880 before any reduction in your benefits. Starting at $41,880, those reductions will be $1 of benefit loss for every $3 above $41,880. Remember, once you hit your normal retirement date, you can earn as much as you wish. It is just in the transition year that you have this potential $1-for-$3 reduction.

There is good news for earnings in your first year of retirement (at full retirement age) — a special rule applies. You should receive a full Social Security check for any whole month you are considered to be retired, regardless of your yearly earnings up to that point. This means that if, at your Social Security retirement date, you also retire from your regular job and take a part-time job or become self-employed, then only the earnings from your part-time job or your self-employment will count toward the calculation of a potential reduction. Again, the earnings in the part-year that lead up to your Social Security retirement date will not be counted.

There is more good news. Your Social Security payments are recalculated to give you credit for the withheld/reduced benefits that were triggered by your pre-retirement work. So at least in theory, the reduction, if any, that you had in your benefits while you continued to work will eventually be made up to you.

You mean I might have to pay taxes on my benefits?

Another consideration for your Social Security benefit decisions are related to income taxes. If your combined income (see definition below) is between $25,000 and $34,000, then up to 50% of your Social Security benefits will be taxed. If your combined income is greater than $34,000, up to 85% of your Social Security benefits will be subject to income tax.

For a married couple, the income limits are $32,000 to $44,000 for the 50% taxable category and over $44,000 for the 85% category.

The term "combined income" is your adjusted gross income plus non-taxable interest plus one half of your Social Security benefits.

While the government is going to "pay you back" for reductions in your Social Security benefits prior to your normal retirement date (if you made too much), with income taxes paid, you never get that money back.

So another factor for determining whether you're going to take your benefits early (age 62), at your normal retirement date (or even later at age 70), may depend on whether those payments will be impacted by the income tax issues.

Income tax strategies to consider:

There are tax strategies that may be applicable to your situation once you retire. For example, you may want to consider converting some IRA accounts over to a Roth IRA since you may not have a drop in taxable income due to your retirement. If you're going to use this type of strategy, however, you probably don't want to start your Social Security payments early and have them be partially taxed as a result of your other tax strategy planning.

Even if you are not doing a Traditional-IRA-to-Roth-IRA strategy, you still may be better off living on your IRA withdrawals instead of starting your Social Security retirement early. If you're going to have to withdraw funds from IRA accounts anyway (due to cash flow needs) that puts you above the Social Security tax thresholds, then you may want to simply withdraw extra IRA funds rather than starting your Social Security retirement early. You are always going to pay income taxes on 100% of a traditional IRA withdrawal. If the IRA withdrawal also triggers a tax on your Social Security benefits, then the effective rate of tax on the IRA withdrawal can be pretty high. By pulling out extra income from IRAs and allowing the deferral of your Social Security retirement benefits, you may eliminate a tax completely (i.e., the tax on your Social Security). In this manner, you eliminate the hidden penalty tax on your Social Security benefits.

Here is a trick that might work (married couples only):

There are several unique tax strategies that you may want to consider. One of those is a strategy for a married couple, both with Social Security retirement benefits. If both husband and wife are about the same age, the strategy is to have the spouse with the higher benefit start his or her benefits at normal retirement age. The other spouse will defer taking his or her benefit until age 70 and instead take a "spousal benefit," which is one half of his or her spouse's retirement benefit, at his or her normal retirement age. By doing this, you get a free extra benefit (one half of the spousal benefit) that you otherwise would not be entitled to if you both begin your retirement at your normal retirement age.

End of Lawyers? That depends. Financial advisors and planners have often been ahead of most lawyers in understanding the ins and outs of Social Security retirement planning. The exception, however, would be an elder law attorney. Experienced elder law attorneys should be well-versed in this area. While there are lawyers with core competence in the Social Security arena, they tend to address disability claims and are usually a different group from estate planning and elder law attorneys. Finally, online technology may actually help lawyers overcome some of their shortfalls of knowledge in area.

CHAPTER 38

At-Home or Nursing Home Care: Medicaid Planning

*How many lawyers does it take
to stop a moving bus?*

Jamie Hargrove

Never enough!

THE END of LAWYERS: *Thank Goodness!*

As I mentioned in Chapter 36, America is getting older at an alarming pace. Of those over age 65, the fastest growing age group is those over the age of 80. According to the U.S. Census Bureau, in 2010 there were more than 11 million Americans over 80. Unfortunately, it has been estimated that of those, as many as half have Alzheimer's or some other form of dementia.

Medicaid is a federal and state-funded program, administered by each state, designed to provide medical care to the needy. Unlike Medicare, Medicaid covers long-term nursing home care. Each state has a certain amount of discretion in determining which services will be provided and who will qualify.

For as long as you qualify for Medicaid, your entire cost of care, including medical needs, nursing home costs, etc., may be covered.

Generally[16], to qualify, you must meet <u>all</u> of the following:

- You are either over age 65, are blind or disabled
- You are admitted to a nursing home for medical reasons pursuant to a doctor's direction
- Your monthly income is within the Medicaid limits, which vary from state to state. Some states are known as "income cap" states, which require that monthly income not exceed $2,199, while other states have more flexible income limits that require you to spend down any income over the threshold (which also vary from state to state).
- You have no more than $2,000 in non-exempt assets
- Your spouse, if any, has no more than $119,220 in non-exempt assets
- You have not made gifts to individuals within the time limitations of the "60-month rule"

16 These rules apply to many states, but certainly not all of them. Each state has its own rules, so you will need to look at your particular state of residence to determine the qualifications that will apply to your situation.

If you apply for Medicaid, you are required to disclose all gifts you made to individuals within the preceding 60 months, hence the term, "60-month rule." Charitable gifts to qualified nonprofit organizations are not included. If you have made such gifts, you will not qualify for Medicaid until the earlier of 1) 60 months after the date of the last gift, or 2) a shorter period computed by dividing the total value of the gifts by the average monthly cost of nursing home services, which is an amount that is set state by state. Currently, those amounts range from $4,000 to $12,112.

Only non-exempt assets are taken into account when determining whether you are eligible. Exempt assets vary from state to state. Some of the more common exemptions include the following:

- Your residence and adjoining property, if owned by the spouse
- An unlimited amount of household goods and personal effects
- $2,000 in any kind of asset for a family size of one, $4,000 for a family size of two
- One wedding ring and one engagement ring
- Prosthetic devices, dialysis machines, hospital beds, wheelchairs and similar equipment
- One automobile if used for employment, to obtain medical treatment, or if specially equipped; otherwise, only equity of $4,500 in an automobile is excluded
- Cash surrender value of life insurance, if less than $1,500
- Burial plots and caskets for immediate family
- Up to $1,500 for burial costs, if specifically set aside for such expenses

- A life interest in real estate or other property
- Health insurance premiums
- Court-ordered support for dependents
- Pension plan interests, IRAs and deferred compensation are excluded as assets but are included under the income test
- Certain annuities if they are actuarially sound (see definitions below)
- Equity of $6,000 in income-producing real estate; the income, however, is not exempt

Federal Medicaid laws allow for "spousal impoverishment" provisions that are designed to preserve and protect your income and resources for the benefit of your spouse should you go on Medicaid. Your spouse can receive part or all of your income as long as his or her income, when combined with your income, does not exceed a specific amount each month. This varies from state to state from less than $2,000 to $3,000.

The use of annuities can be a key tool for Medicaid planning. The use of resources to purchase certain annuities can invoke the "60-month rule," however, if the annuity is not actuarially sound. To be actuarially sound, the expected return on the annuity must be proportionate with the life expectancy of the individual. If the annuity is not actuarially sound, an ineligibility period will be assessed.

A commercial annuity is a product sold by financial institutions designed to grow funds put into it. Then, upon maturity, it pays out a stream of payments to the individual who invested in. Annuities are primarily used to ensure steady cash flow during retirement. Annuities can be structured to consider a wide variety of factors, such as the length of time that payments from the annuity can continue. Annuities can be created so that, upon maturity, payments will continue as long as either the owner or his or her spouse is alive. Annuities can also be structured to pay out funds for a fixed amount of time, such as 20 years, regardless of how long the annuity owner lives.

Another key planning technique centers on ownership of the residence. In most states, the residence, if owned by the spouse, will be an exempt asset. Technically, therefore, you could liquidate a $1 million dollar estate, purchase a $1 million residence and have it transferred to the spouse of the nursing home-bound individual, and if otherwise qualified, be eligible for Medicaid immediately.

If you are married and your spouse is in a nursing home (or likely to be headed there soon), make sure you do not leave your assets to your spouse outright under your will. If you choose to leave assets, use a trust. Otherwise, such an inheritance by your spouse could disqualify him or her from Medicaid eligibility.

If you or your loved one is a veteran, you will want to review the next chapter regarding VA Aid & Attendance benefits. While you generally cannot benefit fully from both programs, it is possible for there to be some short-term benefits of both.[17]

As part of the planning, you will also want to review whom you have named as the executor or executrix under your will, making sure that person is not in a nursing home or likely to be in a nursing home at your death.

Because the residence, if exempt, is generally only exempt when used by the non-nursing home spouse, if the non-nursing home spouse is no longer in the residence, the residence will become a non-exempt resource of the nursing home spouse. Consequently, your will may need to include the handling of your residence.

---

17 Once you qualify for Medicaid benefits, your ability to take advantage of VA Aid & Attendance benefits are significantly limited, if not eliminated. The exception may be for the spouse of the Medicaid recipient. The spouse may still qualify for VA Aid & Attendance benefits. The VA benefits may also be used during spend-down periods.

With the baby boom bubble just now hitting the mid- to upper 60s, the home healthcare, assisted living and nursing home industry is booming and projected to continue to grow for the foreseeable future. Unfortunately for consumers, with such huge demand and a limited supply, such services are not anticipated to be a bargain anytime soon. If anything, those costs will continue to escalate.

Many families are faced with the prospect of completely depleting an estate in a matter of just a few years. Of course, the worst situation is when a husband or wife requires these costly services that deplete an estate and leave the healthy spouse with little or no assets with which to live out his or her life.

The good news is that there are planning opportunities to address these issues and protect the family's assets from being exhausted.

Some families are reluctant to do this type of planning because of a moral or ethical issue. Since my background is in tax planning, I view this situation along those lines. Certainly, if your accountant advises you to take certain steps to minimize your income taxes or reduce liability, you would take his or her advice. Few people would think that working within tax laws to pay less tax is an immoral or unethical practice. When you're dealing with laws related to Medicaid, VA Aid & Attendance (for more on this, see Chapter 39) and other programs, the approach should be no different. With tax planning, you are reducing the government coffers by not paying them as much. With elder care planning, you are reducing the government coffers by asking them to pay you or your caregivers. Either way, the government coffers are reduced when you take advantage of the laws that Congress enacted.

The most well-known planning technique deals with Medicaid. When I first started practicing in the mid-1980s, you could create a Medicaid qualifying trust and, in many states, transfer unlimited assets to it and immediately qualify for government assistance. For the right type of planning, there was no look-back period. Over the years, Congress and state governments have chipped away at that type of planning, so today it is much more restrictive. But planning opportunities still exist, and a trained attorney can help you take advantage of them.

End of Lawyers? Depends. This area of law is continuing to change, and the changes will bring about creativity and efficiency in elder law. There are certainly advisors in this area who are not attorneys but may be very qualified to assist with Medicaid issues. Individuals who do not immediately qualify for Medicaid and need to create a legal plan to position themselves to qualify may require the assistance of an elder law attorney. When legal services are required, elder law attorneys will continue to be an important component of planning that involves government assistance.

CHAPTER 39

Veterans Only: VA Aid & Attendance Planning

What's the difference between a law firm and a circus?

Jamie Hargrove

*At a circus, the clowns don't charge
the public by the hour.*

When it comes to assistance for individuals over age 65 who need at-home, assisted living or nursing home care, there has been no greater secret kept by the federal government than benefits available to wartime veterans, called "VA Aid & Attendance." It seems that Congress created a significant and meaningful benefit to veterans, but because they didn't really want to spend the money, they created legislation that has kept many veterans from "getting the memo."

It goes without saying that you can't expect the government to inform you when you are eligible for certain benefits. A savvy lawyer could make sure you are aware of all the benefits you are entitled to, but most lawyers have been pretty clueless in this particular area until recently. Of course, "most lawyers" doesn't include experienced elder law attorneys. The problem is that the number of such knowledgeable attorneys, while growing, is miniscule in comparison to the demand and opportunity for this benefit.

So, what did Congress do to effectively "hide the ball" on this type of benefit? Well, to Congress' credit, it's not entirely politicians' fault. The resulting impact of their legislation was not foreseen. They actually had the best intentions in mind; they just didn't think it through as well as they should have. Congress effectively made it illegal to take a fee for advising or processing VA Aid & Attendance benefit claims. This, of course, means that if no one can earn a fee, then no one is around to advise veterans of their rights and opportunities unless the government does so itself. Unfortunately, the government does not seem to be stepping in to correct this situation and educate veterans.

One result of this legislation is that some annuity salesmen across the country have realized that they can make a fee off of their annuity sales, then roll the cost of consulting and the application fees for VA benefits into the profit they make on their annuities. (See Chapter 27 for a definition of annuities.) Because annuities, however, are generally small and do not generate a significant enough profit on their own, financial advisors who sell them also are providing consulting services. A common model, therefore, is an annuity sale and consulting arrangement with the agreement that the actual work handled via the application process is at no charge.

Attorneys seem to have an easier path toward combining these services. This is particularly true if they are not selling annuity products.

Bottom line, the government seems to have it out for individuals who sell annuity products in this type of planning. This is unfortunate because annuities can play an important role here. On the other hand, the government's attitude is somewhat justified in that there are some "planners" in this area who offer an annuity as the sole solution. While annuities are important, they are not always the best solution. The key is to associate with reputable financial advisors and the companies they represent.

The VA Aid & Attendance benefit can exceed $30,000 for a husband and wife who are both veterans. This is an annual, recurring payment for as long as both veterans are in need of "aid and attendance." As long as their assets remain at the levels the government allows, and they continue to have a need for assistance (either at home, assisted living or a nursing home), then such benefits should continue.

As of the writing of this book the benefits were as follows:

Status	Monthly Benefit	Annual Benefit
Single veteran	$1,732	$20,784
Married veteran	$2,054	$24,648
Married veteran couple	$2,676	$32,112
Surviving spouse	$1,113	$13,356

In many respects, VA Aid & Attendance planning is very similar to Medicaid planning. It is need-based. The goal of both Medicaid and VA Aid & Attendance is to provide a benefit to individuals who otherwise would not have the financial means to secure home care, assisted living or nursing home care on their own. The key differences in the two programs, however, are significant. They are as follows:

- Medicaid has a 5-year "look back." Currently, VA planning does not have a look-back period. Congress has proposed that this type of planning be subject to a similar look back, but as of the writing of this book, that legislation has not been passed.

- In most states, Medicaid planning has historically not provided for in-home care and assisted living. While that is changing, VA Aid & Attendance clearly provides for both. I think the folks drafting the legislation for VA Aid & Attendance figured out sooner than the Medicaid folks that creating a system that encourages moving people into a nursing home (where services are paid by the government) was not a particularly good system from the government's standpoint. At-home care and assisted living care is a much less expensive alternative, and the government would save a lot of money by paying for those less expensive services.

While these are the two most significant differences between VA Aid & Attendance and Medicaid planning, there are a few other differences. Some of them make it a little more challenging if you are trying to qualify for the VA Aid & Attendance benefit as well as start the 5-year time clock on Medicaid planning. Certainly, both opportunities should be considered before deciding on a plan.

There is a need to coordinate VA and Medicaid[18] planning because some situations that qualify an individual for VA Aid & Attendance benefits may disqualify that person from Medicaid benefits for several years. However, a Medicaid plan will likely qualify for VA Aid & Attendance.

As discussed in Chapter 38 related to Medicaid planning, the use of certain annuities in such planning can be very beneficial. In both types of plans, the use of an annuity must be based on the life expectancy of the individual. This is referred to as an "actuarial" determined annuity. There are some companies, although not many, that have designed products specifically for this market.

An alternative to the public annuity that is most often used in this type of planning is a private annuity. A private annuity is simply an annuity between the individual/insured and a third-party company or individual. It is a contractual obligation that can be designed to qualify for a VA or Medicaid benefit program. The advantage with a private annuity is that, if there is a windfall to the annuity provider and the annuity provider is your own family, it creates a nice planning opportunity. An elder law attorney would need to create and oversee a private annuity arrangement.

End of Lawyers? Depends. VA Aid & Attendance planning is a great opportunity for wartime veterans. It's an ever-changing area, so experienced advisors in this area are key. A good financial advisor with a specialty in this area may be all you need. Like with Medicaid planning, however, if a legal plan is required to re-title assets or create legal documents or vehicles to accomplish the planning, you'll want to engage an attorney.

---

18 Refer to Footnote 17 in Chapter 38 discussing limitations on securing both Medicaid and VA Aid & Attendance benefits.

SOMETHING TO CONSIDER

CHAPTER 40

I'll Have Another Home Please (Wealth and Its Stress)

What's the difference between a lawyer and a terrorist?

Jamie Hargrove

You can negotiate with a terrorist.

As an estate planning attorney, I get to experience life from a lot of different perspectives — my very interesting clients' perspectives. When you deal with highly successful people, you also have the opportunity to see first-hand how their decisions, some relating to their estate plans and some just to their lifestyles, impact them both negatively and positively. In this and the next two chapters, I offer some observations, views and opinions that I have gleaned over the years from my clients.

My first observation relates to wealth, its by-products and the stress it can bring. One of the greatest stress points for a lot of people is time management. If you think about it, every decision you make can have a dramatic impact on your time. You want to know why many wealthy people are not happy? Too often, it is because they have never learned the correlation between decisions (many times, decision to buy stuff) and time management.

When you decided to put your son or daughter in tee ball, that decision created a time commitment. When you later decided to put the same child in soccer, basketball or track, you made yet another set of decisions that involved allocations of time. Just like decisions we make later in life about what we do with our money, we seldom think about the time that will inevitably go into each of those decisions. The point, of course, is that we learn bad habits of over-commitment early on.

As we get wealthier, the decision whether to buy that company or to make an investment in those apartments becomes more of an issue of whether it's a good deal rather than what impact it will have on our time.

What about that second, or even third, home? Do those bring happiness to one's life? Well, certainly in some cases they do. But in too many cases, they only bring an allocation of additional time we didn't have to spare. So what happens? We suddenly create not only financial stress, but stress on our time, which can have just as negative an impact as the financial stress. Lack of time to do the things that we've committed to do is one of the greatest problems we create for ourselves.

Maybe you want to buy a larger home because you've just had triplets. In fact, because you've just had triplets, you need to build a home so it's exactly what you need to accommodate a unique and rapidly expanding family. Now think about this. If you have just had three new children enter your family, do you really think that you have a spare moment to deal with all of the decisions involved in building a new home? Is this really the time to do that? Does your life not have enough stress already? Where are you going to find the time, and who is going to suffer as a result of adding one more item to your already extremely busy schedule?

One of my favorite illustrations of this issue involves the purchase of a vacation home. For many years, my clients, a lovely couple, would take off two months in the spring to go fishing at a favorite destination. They rented a nice place there that they loved.

In the years when their business was growing, they just never seemed to have enough capital to buy a vacation home. That extra capital was always put back into the business. Even though they could have gotten a loan to buy a property, they didn't want to risk the added debt.

They sold their business for a lot of money just as they reached retirement age. As a result, they could buy that vacation home and pay cash, and they did just that.

I used to do gift tax returns for this couple, and around the time they were finishing up their two-month fishing vacation, I would inquire as to how the fishing was coming along. And for every year they had the rental property, inevitably the response was the same: "We fish from sun up until sun down, and we are having a ball!"

I can still remember the first time I called after they had purchased their new property. It was right at the end of their latest vacation. The husband answered the phone, and I asked him how the fishing was this year. To my surprise, the response came back, "Oh! We haven't been fishing yet." I was shocked. He told me, "We've been remodeling a part of our new home, and we've been looking for furniture, so we just haven't had time to go fishing." The next year, they were dealing with some storm damage. The next year it seemed like it was something else. Before they owned that second home, they were able to enjoy a glorious vacation. After they purchased their lovely vacation home, the stress of ownership and the time constraints of maintaining that home had all but zapped the joy of what used to be a wonderful two months of relaxation.

Of course, some people would relish the chance to buy and remodel a second home. Some of them might even consider that type of project a vacation from their daily lives. If that's what energizes you, buying a second home may not cause added stress. Just remember that virtually every decision you make requires an allocation of time. Your question, then, must be whether such allocation of time will be toward something that produces joy and happiness or something that simply produces more stress.

End of Lawyers? Not really. Everything is not about dollars and cents, or trusts and investments. Having an experienced lawyer who has worked with others in similar situations can provide you with invaluable feedback and advice. So, this is probably not the area to trade your attorney in for an online experience.

CHAPTER 41

The Happiest People I Know: Generous Givers

What do honest lawyers and UFOs have in common?

Jamie Hargrove

You always hear about them,
but you never see them.

I love my law practice. For over 30 years, I have been blessed to collaborate with some of the most creative, intelligent, innovative and downright nice clients, as well as their other advisors. While in those 30 years, I may have had a handful of clients who I didn't like (and vice versa), for the most part I've had a fantastic client base.

I have seen very well-educated people do creative and innovative things to capitalize on their educational foundation. On the other hand, I've also had some wonderfully innovative, highly intelligent clients who have mastered extraordinary business skills, despite a lack of formal education. I have witnessed secretaries and low-paid educators — through simple lifestyles and shrewd investing — become millionaires.

While I certainly have my share of clients who own big homes, expensive cars and an airplane or two, my practice has mostly been made up of "the millionaire next door."

When people ask me, "Of all the clients you have, of all the varied backgrounds they come from and the varied successes they each have had, who are your happiest clients?" The answer to that question is simple, straightforward and consistent across virtually my entire client base: Outward focus, outward focus, outward focus!

If there is one common thread among my happy clients, it seems to be that the individuals who have an outward focus to their lives are the ones who are most content. In many cases, that outward focus is toward charitable or religious causes. In other cases, it's on a business where the betterment of employees is as important as making a profit. Having a passion for something other than making money and accumulating personal wealth and luxuries is an attribute that goes a long way toward bringing about contentment, fulfillment and happiness.

So, you might wonder what this chapter has to do with estate planning. It actually has a lot to do with estate planning when you stop to think what it's really about. Estate planning often is about ensuring your own financial security (and yes, in theory, the resulting happiness) and then devising a plan to pass that financial security (also, in theory, happiness) to the next generation or several generations. I never met a client who told me he wanted to leave his estate to his family in such a way as to make them *unhappy.* Just the contrary, most clients are very intent on "doing it right," which to them means happy, secure kids and grandkids. But most realize that while simply saving taxes or setting up a trust may bring financial security, it isn't necessarily going to guarantee happiness and joy. As a part of the estate planning discussion, it is important to discuss the emotional aspects of the process, because they can shape the way in which an estate plan is set up and administered.

My wife and I love to attend a national conference on generous giving (www.generousgiving.org). It's a two-day conference focused on — you guessed it — generous giving. The Generous Giving organization is underwritten by the Maclellan Foundation based in Chattanooga, Tennessee, which has provided tremendous support for great causes all around the world. In its fifth generation, it has touched the lives of so many people that it would be impossible to count them all. You know an act is genuine when a person does something for you and you cannot do something for them in return. That's the way the Generous Giving organization was set up. Its operating costs are completely funded by the Maclellan Foundation, and they do not accept donations. They spend a lot of time and effort encouraging you to give of your time, money and other resources to other charitable causes, yet make it very clear that they don't want your money themselves. They will take your volunteer time, but never as a means toward fundraising. Because of that very uniqueness, strong leadership and the wonderful financial backing of the Maclellan Foundation, it has made for a very unusual, yet very effective organization.

The focus of the conference is to encourage people to become generous givers and to offer support to those who already do so. The organization shares stories of the joy that giving brings, not about giving to simply get more. This is not a "prosperity gospel" that some TV evangelists advocate. This is simply to encourage those of the Christian faith to seek and find true joy and happiness through generous giving. Regardless of your faith, I have seen the tremendous positive impact generous giving can have on the lives of those who give. Obviously, the recipient of the gift can see his or her life changed, but where I see the real transformation is in the lives of the givers themselves.

Generous giving is a journey, not an end. While there are entire books written on this subject, for now, you'll have to rely on my 30 years of experience with people from all socio-economic backgrounds: Generous giving makes a difference.

End of Lawyers? No, you certainly don't need an attorney to be a generous giver. A skilled estate planning lawyer, however, can help craft a plan that fits your goals for the legacy you want to create for your estate.

CHAPTER 42

This Too Shall Pass: Family Care, Long-term Care Insurance, Etc.

*Why does California
have the most attorneys,*

*and New Jersey have the most
toxic waste dumps?*

Jamie Hargrove

New Jersey got first pick.

One of the reasons people become motivated to plan their estates is over concern that if they don't, their families may not be able to come to an agreement once they are gone. The last thing most people want is for controversy over an inheritance, healthcare, or a host of other issues to rip the family apart. Too often, I have watched these family conflicts unfold, and I don't want it to happen to others. One issue that often causes conflict is over the care of Mom and Dad as they become elderly. Understanding some of those dynamics can help you as make decisions in your own planning.

The title for this chapter, "This Too Shall Pass," came, with permission, via the title of one of my favorite books by Ginny Sisk of Lexington, Kentucky. If you are dealing with some of the issues I address in this chapter, you will certainly want to pick up a copy of Ginny's book.

In her book, she details the struggles she experienced as one of several siblings caring for an aging parent. When you have multiple people in multiple situations, the family dynamics of dealing with the problems of aging parents can be challenging at best.

One of the interesting aspects of Ginny's book is that she was a godly wife of a very prominent Southern Baptist preacher who pastored one of the largest Baptist churches in Central Kentucky. She was known as a kind, loving, thoughtful person. Yet when you read some of the emotions and challenges she went through with her family, you discover that even people strong in their faith who have a compassionate attitude can have their loving spirit tested when it comes to caring for a loved one and the issues that can arise among the family.

When it comes to family members "taking their turn" at helping with Mom or Dad, remember that virtually no one is sitting around doing nothing. Everyone has busy lives, even if they are not high-level executives doing business all across the country. While you think the imposition would be more significant for you because of your busy business schedule, it really is no more of an inconvenience than for your farmer brother or your stay-at-home sister. Their schedules are no less busy and no less important. You cannot assume, therefore, that they are going to roll up their sleeves, jump in and take over the care of your parents simply because they don't have plane tickets booked or conference calls scheduled.

An easy solution is to just let Mom move in with one of your siblings. While that can work sometimes, it's rarely a long-term fix. While it makes caregiving more convenient, the caregiving itself still takes a lot of time. If you've ever been a stay-at-home mom or dad, you will remember at the end of the day you wondered why you got little to nothing done other than taking care of your child. Having an elderly parent in your home can be no different.

If your sibling is taking Mom or Dad into their home, consider yourself very fortunate. Also don't forget that this is a major inconvenience! Do everything in your power to help give your brother or sister some relief. Make long visits, and let your brother or sister get out of the house. Move in for the weekend, and let your brother or sister take a vacation. Every day, remind yourself that your sibling is being inconvenienced. Hopefully, that will encourage you to look for ways to offset some of the major commitment that your brother or sister has made for the well-being of your mom or dad.

Have you ever heard Mom or Dad say they never want to go to a nursing home and leave their own home? Well, if you haven't, you would be in the minority. In over 30 years of practice, most of my elderly clients have told me that it was a priority to stay in their own home. It really doesn't matter how small or modest their home may be compared to your home or a wonderful assisted living facility. That's their home, and any other place won't do. One of the reasons for the huge increase in the number and size of home health organizations is because

Mom and Dad want to stay in their own home.

If Mom and Dad need care of any type, you owe it to yourself and to your parents to get an assessment by a professional home care organization. The home assessments are usually free, they can help determine whether there are any government benefits or programs that your parents may qualify for, and they can fit their services to your budget. If you have a family member staying with your parents or your parents have moved in with a family member, simply having an at-home organization come in for a few hours a day a few times a week can be a huge benefit. While those services are not inexpensive, they can significantly increase not only Mom and Dad's quality of life, but that of the family as well.

Even if you decide that you do not need those services immediately, you can prepare yourself for what could happen in case of a fall or illness that creates an immediate need for care. It will be handy for your home health organization to already have your parents' information on file so they can respond quickly when an emergency occurs.

I've already mentioned it above, but you cannot over-communicate among your family members. Even if you're scattered across the country, everyone has a cell phone that has speakerphone or conferencing capabilities. Learn how to maximize your phone's features, and if the caregiver family member does not have such a phone, chip in and buy him or her one that will allow the family a chance to regularly check in. There is also other technology available through tablets and video conferencing services. If you don't know how to use Skype™ or FaceTime®, it's time to learn.

This is not a time for the caregiver family member to be isolated from the rest of the family. He needs continued encouragement from the rest of the family, as well as an outlet for all the problems and issues he has to handle. Sometimes he simply needs a platform to release his frustrations. I've seen busy, empty-nest moms with both paid and volunteer jobs suddenly have a complete change of priorities with the birth of a grandchild. The joy of spending time with that precious grandchild offsets the loss of income or loss of involvement with organizations that had become important to her. As you look at caring for Mom and Dad, consider that adapting to their needs is the same type of lifestyle change. Your parents won't be around forever, and this may simply be your opportunity to slow down and focus on what's really important.

OK, now that you have read the above suggestions, think about these issues for your own planning. You should ask yourself what you can do with your own planning to make sure you minimize family discontent. One of the most important issues to address is long-term care insurance. Do you need to consider long-term care insurance? If you are insurable, absolutely.

Having long-term care insurance can go a long way toward dealing with family conflicts. Even when an elderly person has adequate finances, getting him or her to use them can be challenging. When "someone else is paying," you would be amazed at how attitudes about care can change.

You may think your situation will be different. And maybe if your kids aren't married, they might. But there is a pretty good chance that your son-in-law and/or daughter-in-law is not going to be all that excited about caring for you — particularly so if you have the finances to do so but are viewed as "too cheap" to pay for your own care.

You insure your home and car, shouldn't you also ensure that your family stays together and that you are properly taken care of? That is what long-term care insurance does, and you need to get it.

Should you draft your healthcare documents in such a way as to address some of these issues? Absolutely. As I have mentioned several times in this book, estate planning is as much about creating family harmony and happiness as it is about financial security and taxes.

End of Lawyers? Probably. An experienced lawyer can help address your unique family situation and prepare for issues that might create future conflict if not properly considered now. An experienced financial planner/advisor, however, can be your go-to person. He or she can be just as well equipped to address these issues and, of course, would likely be able to better address issues related to long-term care insurance.

FINAL WORDS

CHAPTER 43

The End of Lawyers

What's the definition of mixed emotions?

Watching your attorney drive over a cliff in your new Ferrari.

If you've read much of this book, hopefully you now have a greater appreciation for attorneys, and especially their role in estate planning. You might even disagree with Shakespeare's "Henry VI, Part 2," where Dick the butcher uttered the famous words, "First thing we do, let's kill all the lawyers."

Contrary to this book's title, it was not about getting rid of (all) lawyers, just some of them — the inefficient ones with little or no appreciation for customer service. It's about the need for lawyers to be more efficient in offering legal services and about consumers of legal services being more educated before they engage a lawyer.

Software systems are readily available today to help lawyers practice more efficiently. Unfortunately, lawyers tend to do things the way they've always done them. For too many of them, that has not produced a very efficient practice. When you combine the inefficiency of many lawyers with an uneducated consumer, the result is not very promising.

This book is ultimately about educating you as a consumer about legal services. It's also for lawyers who may not specialize in estate planning, but need the information in this book to supplement a general understanding of various estate planning topics and issues.

At the end of the day, for a financial advisor, a consumer of legal services, an attorney practicing outside of an exclusive estate planning practice or someone at a charity, university or foundation, knowledge is power. While part of this book is about DIY (do-it-yourself) services, unfortunately there are many areas in this field of practice that are simply going to require the guidance of a trained, and often specialized, attorney. Hopefully this book has helped you identify some of the questions and issues related to estate planning where you might need to engage a professional.

Just finding an attorney can be challenging. Using sites like NetLaw and other online legal services, you should be able to select from attorneys based on their bios, fee arrangements and, in some cases, reviews from others just like you. Consumer reviews by people who have actually used the services of the listed attorneys have been missing on most lawyer-referral sites. I believe that having access to attorney ratings by consumers is key to not only finding good, efficient attorneys, but also to providing an incentive for attorneys to step up their game.

As important as the topics in this book are, it concerns me that so many people have not done any estate planning to protect their families and/or businesses. This is an area of the law that should not be so easily avoided or delayed. Most of us, as natural procrastinators, just never get around to things that are important but don't seem urgent. I hope this book has not only given you some meaningful information, but also a sense of urgency to get your affairs, both personal and business, in order.